The Making of the
BRITISH COUNTRYSIDE

The Making of the
BRITISH COUNTRYSIDE

Ron Freethy

DAVID & CHARLES
Newton Abbot   London   North Pomfret (Vt)

British Library Cataloguing in Publication Data

Freethy, Ron
    The Making of the British Countryside
    1. Ecology
    I. Title
    574.5   QH541

ISBN 0-7153-8012-5

Library of Congress Catalog Card Number: 80-68688

Typeset in 10 on 12 point Century by
Typesetters (Birmingham) Limited
and printed in Great Britain
by Butler & Tanner Limited, Frome and London
for David & Charles (Publishers) Limited
Brunel House Newton Abbot Devon

Published in the United States of America
by David & Charles Inc
North Pomfret Vermont 05053 USA

Contents

Introduction

We know that man's activities affect our wildlife. But how and why is this so? In order to plan for the future we must take into account both past and present situations.

Woodlands once covered the whole of Britain and so were our principal habitat for wildlife; their future must be a matter of the utmost concern. They have been fragmented, mainly by man but also to some extent by climatic variations. On the whole most forms of woodland wildlife except the trees themselves thrive best on the edges of the woods, or in the clearings, where the essential light energy can penetrate. A hedge is really a woodland edge without the wood, a field is a clearing minus the woodland. Both these are important habitats for wildlife and their future is of great importance.

The effects of man's increasing and understandable demand for industrial, domestic and aesthetic water are another powerful influence on animals and plants — looked at in Chapter 5. Our needs for water impose great strain upon the wildlife of our watercourses and water catchment areas. One solution to the problem is the creation of large upland reservoirs, either by damming valleys or altering existing lakes; this leads naturally to a discussion of the problems encountered by wildlife in upland regions. Increasing numbers of walkers, as people now have more leisure time, are flocking to the high hills. They are often oblivious of rare plants beneath their feet or the birds above their heads which are unable to return to their eggs until the visitors have departed.

No two environments seem to be in sharper contrast than a moorland and a seashore and yet they face just the same problem — too many people at the wrong time of year. Chapter 7 examines the coastline of Britain, which is one of the richest in Europe, supporting a wide range of plants and animals. It also attracts hordes of holidaymakers who demand camping and caravan sites, hotels and all the trappings associated with 'having a good time'. The solution must be one of compromise between the right of individuals to enjoy themselves and the equally important right of our wild things to be allowed to survive.

The impression sometimes given by naturalists is that our wildlife is incapable of fighting back, that the future for most animals and some plants is hopeless. This is just not true and in the final chapter the resilience of nature is discussed. Even in the centres of our largest cities mammals such as foxes roam free, insects continue to evolve ingenious survival strategies, flowers bloom and trees provide song posts for a healthy, if selective, bird population.

By looking at just a few typical species from each habitat in some detail, we can begin to see the situation, the ecological problems and possibilities, for each habitat. The whole book is concerned with the way Britain's fauna and flora have continued to thrive despite the very considerable changes brought about — not only today but also, if more gradually, in the past — by man. Now that the word 'conservation' seems to be understood, perhaps for the first time, we should look forward to the future with confidence. This is true, however, only if we are ever alert, and every would-be intrusion into a valuable habitat is warded off unless it is entirely unavoidable. If our wildlife can be as healthy as it is, despite what man has done to it, what momentous progress could be made with just a little more help from us.

This book is for, and dedicated to, all those who love to watch the wildlife of Britain as much as I do.

1
Woodland: the Basic Habitat

They shut the road through the woods
Seventy years ago.
Weather and rain have undone it again
And now you would never know
There was once a road through the woods.

Woodland is the natural vegetation of Britain, so that is where most of our wildlife used to live. Yet Kipling's lines above record a reversal of man's usual practice. From prehistoric times onward, and during the last 5,000 years at an ever-accelerating rate, he has made inroads into the indigenous forest, exerting a profound influence on its wildlife; some of its inhabitants have become extinct in the process, and others have been added, sometimes from distant lands.

The history of woodlands in Britain is indeed a complex story of the interactions of climate, soil type, slope and altitude, but above all of often thoughtless interference by man — which can be traced as far back as about 12,000 BC.

Twelve thousand years ago the last Ice Age reluctantly slackened its grip, having ground out valleys, and transported soils and even huge boulders over considerable distances. It was on this canvas that the tapestry of our woodlands was woven. When the last of the ice-sheets disappeared from lowland Britain between 12,000 and 10,000 BC, they left behind them extensive lakes and meres, but also a vast area of low-lying wetlands. This has been called the 'late glacial period' and had its own unique and very hardy flora.

These conditions were obviously unsuitable for the growth of trees, but the climate was rapidly improving, marshland began to dry out, and with the onset of this period, known as the 'pre-boreal', conditions for tree growth improved. Britain was still at this time connected to the continent by a land bridge. Our Thames was a feeder tributary to a huge River Rhine meandering its way through a soggy plain. The dominant tree at this period was birch, but also present were hazel, oak, elm and in a few places alder — a natural history unravelled by the painstaking work of modern scientists. The technique of pollen

analysis was developed in the 1920s by a Swedish botanist, Lagerheim. British scientists were not slow to follow the initiative, and the history of British vegetation is still being unravelled. It has been discovered that most species of flowering plant produce pollen grains of a unique shape, and furthermore the cell wall of these grains is almost indestructible, even if treated with concentrated acids, which would never be encountered in the natural environment of the plant. Most trees are wind-pollinated, the grains being light enough to be carried quite long distances. Some germinate, others fall on stony ground and some are deposited in boggy areas and become incorporated in the peat.

This black soggy-looking stuff is as vital to fuel the research fires of the botanist as it is to warm the bodies of many northern folk in winter. Those who sit by a fragrant fire of dried peat may forget that it consists of partly decomposed plants, particularly those which normally thrive in boglands such as cotton grasses (*Eriophorum* spp) and bog mosses (*Sphagnum* spp). Living material will not decay completely in the absence of oxygen, since the bacteria which break it down are unable to respire; so in cold and waterlogged areas decay is halted. As pollen grains carried in by the wind become incorporated into the sinking vegetation, layer upon layer will form, and unless some great upheaval occurs the peat will represent a chronological record of past vegetation. If the age of each layer of peat is worked out, the vegetational history of the area can be described. Scientists are able to do this with a fair degree of accuracy by a technique known as radio-carbon dating.

By 7500 BC Britain was enjoying a warm and dry phase averaging some 2°C above what we are experiencing at present. This pleasant 'boreal period' lasted for some 2,000 years. Pine became almost as common as birch, but eventually was replaced by extensive growth of English elm and oak which dominated vast areas. During the whole of the boreal period, land levels were sinking and allowing the encroaching sea to erode away the land bridges separating Britain from the Continent of Europe. At the conclusion of the period Britain was an island. Evidence supporting the contention that the land beneath the Channel was once able to support vast areas of trees is not difficult to come by. Stumps of many species have been dredged up by ships laying cables or surveying the sea floor.

The human population at this time were nomadic hunters who made few permanent demands upon their environment. They have left flint implements, identified by archaeologists as a product of mesolithic cultures.

The old road through the woods—Roanhead, near Askam-in-Furness, Cumbria

The period of relatively high rainfall, with fairly high temperatures, that occurred in Britain from around 5,500 BC — 'the Atlantic period' — was characterised by a phenomenal increase in alder, as the woodlands became damper, although oak was still the dominant tall tree. Pine diminished over considerable areas, although it seems to have held its own, at least to some extent, in Scotland. Hazel was still the dominant understorey shrub, a position which it still holds. It was during this period that the first change in man's attitude to his environment can be detected. He began to take an interest in agriculture. For the first time trees were under threat. The mesolithic culture was slowly superseded by that of the neolithic people, who possessed much-improved flint implements and could create clearings in which to keep animals in a state of at least semi-domestication, and primitive crops began to be grown.

It has been observed that a flint hand-axe is hardly a match for a huge oak, but people were probably not then in a hurry. Any large tree in the way was simply bark-ringed, thus cutting off the water supply between root and leaf, and interrupting the food supply flowing in the reverse direction. These people did not know how the tree was killed, only that this was a way of removing an obstacle without a great deal of physical labour. This was the beginning of a period of domination by the pastoralists, which continues today. The natural characteristics of vegetation are obviously determined by climate, but this has been considerably and increasingly modified since the Atlantic period by the activities of *Homo sapiens.*

The Atlantic period was succeeded by the so-called sub-boreal period, which had a much more profound effect on the vegetation of mainland Europe than on our own offshore island. That it was a dry period is clearly demonstrated in the pollen analysis: pine dramatically recovered and elm and lime correspondingly declined. There is evidence of a further extension of agricultural practices, shown by a rise in the proportion of cereal-crop pollen found in the peat deposits of the period. Also, charcoal deposits embedded in the peat indicate that some clearance was made by burning.

During this time the working of metals spread from Near Eastern civilisations. This process commenced about 4000 BC but it took time for what is now known as the Bronze Age to reach Britain; it flourished from about 2000 BC and lasted for some 1,500 years. It appears that the climate became too dry for human populations to survive on the summits of upland slopes and civilisations tended to become centred in the damper lowland areas. These drier conditions proved much to the liking of the beech, and to a lesser extent the

Pollen grains: A alder, B birch, C oak, D hazel, E pine

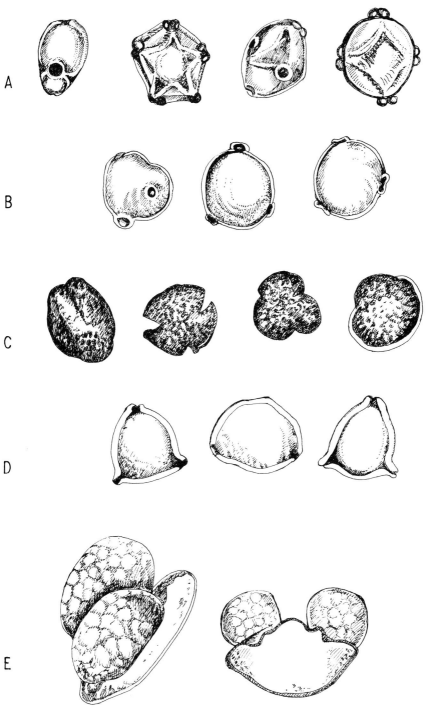

Site of iron-age fort at Grassington, Yorks

hornbeam, both of which still flourish on well-drained soils in the south of England; but the lime all but became extinct.

It did manage to survive, however, and in due time the climate once more deteriorated, becoming considerably wetter and cooler. In the so-called sub-Atlantic period the lime recovered, pine receded, and the tough old oak went majestically on with the process of staying alive as if nothing had changed. In fact we are *still* in the midst of this sub-Atlantic period. It began just after 1000 BC and any fluctuations since have been relatively minor.

The onset of the sub-Atlantic period of the botanist more or less coincides with what historians have called the Iron Age. The discovery of the process whereby iron could be smelted made possible the development of tools tough enough to allow forest destruction on a grand scale. When the Iron Age forts were constructed, almost totally of wood, usually on the summits of hills, large areas around must have been cleared of any timber which might hinder the defenders from detecting the approach of strangers. The remains of many such forts probably lie hidden beneath the undergrowth of many of our regenerated woodlands (yes, there are a few!).

During the Iron Age, huge areas of Southern England began to be cultivated. Much of Wiltshire (what is now Salisbury Plain) and the Dorset uplands were cleared. These districts have now grassed over, and regeneration has been prevented by grazing livestock, but the 'lynchets' (earth banks) still delineate the ancient fields.

At the time of Julius Caesar's invasion of Britain the indigenous Celts had evolved sophisticated wheeled ploughs, capable not only of producing sufficient corn for home consumption but also a surplus for export. Thus Ancient Britain's 'balance of payments' was healthy. The wholesale destruction of woodland without doubt increased during the Roman Occupation, but the really damaging acceleration did not come until the Romans had gone home to attend to the pressing domestic problems of their own decaying society, and the Angles and Saxons arrived to occupy the vacant niche. These new arrivals were long-established and highly efficient cultivators, possessing also courage and military technology. Their superior weaponry drove the Celts northward and westward, and the Saxons soon set about the task of clearing the woodlands from the valleys. Britain was now becoming pastoral. Then from the ninth century onwards, mostly in the north of England, the Danes began to alter British lives, culture and landscape, destroying areas of woodland to satisfy their building requirements, domestic and military.

Not only the human population, but also that of grazing stock was increasing. As trees were cleared, the underlying soil, fertilised by centuries of leaf mould, was deep and fertile, and yielded much more productive pasture land than the upland fields used hitherto. This intense cropping prevented regeneration of woodland and Britain's vegetational overcoat was by this time decidedly worn. When William of Normandy arrived in Britain in 1066, fresh from the densely afforested continent, he was obviously appalled by the lack of trees: for it has been estimated that by this time some 80 per cent of our woodland had gone. William's Domesday Survey of 1086 revealed the stark reality of the wood shortage, and even in those days it was realised that something would have to be done. Royal 'forests' were set up over which the King had total control — many of these so-called forests, of which the New Forest in Hampshire is best known, were in open country, cleared of trees, over which the King could hunt; since the hunt passed through a given area so seldom, some degree of regeneration was obviously possible. Norman rule may have been harsh and social injustices rife, but this was a period of some slight recovery of vegetation. The same cannot be said for the woodland fauna and many of Britain's native woodland mammals were on the brink of extinction; woodland herbivores such as the red deer were obliged to quit and literally head for the hills. One animal already

Red deer

under the sentence of death during this period was the wolf.

Man's primeval fear of these slinking, mysterious beasts gave hero-status to those who could rid an area of them. The tale of Little Red Riding Hood's travels through the forest may well have come from these days. Wolf-hunting was a popular sport throughout Europe, and Saxon literature abounds with tales of fearsome wolves and of the fearless wolfhounds which assisted hunters. Alfred was by all accounts a better hand at wolf-hunting than at cake-watching, which added to the respect afforded him by his subjects. The Saxon culture was so permeated with the hunt that their month corresponding to our January was called Wolfmonat – Wolf month, the animal's vulnerable cubbing period. Wolves require more food at this time and so the superstitious human population considered itself more liable to attack than during other periods.

Despite the hunting pressure, wolves managed to survive in fair numbers by diving for cover, and lurking deep in the shade of the wildwood, holed up beneath the gnarled roots of an old oak. Lone travellers through the trees went in constant fear: whether such fears were real or imaginary is a matter for conjecture, but the fact remains that in parts of northern England refuges were provided in lonely

Wolf

places, constructed stoutly enough to keep out hungry wolves — which presumably lacked the lung capacity to 'huff and puff and blow the house down'. These refuges were called spittals, a name still associated with place names in Northumberland, Yorkshire and Scotland. A hole was often left in the building for the occupants to see where the wolves were. From these 'lupus holes' we get the phrase 'loop-hole'.

According to the *Book of St Albans*, published in 1486, a year after the Tudor dynasty took over the helm of England, there appears to have been a significant shift in attitudes to wolf-hunting. Here for the first time we find a close season mentioned. The law may well have been in force for some years before publication, but the date is significant nevertheless. Hunting the wolf was only permitted from 25 December to 25 March, which suggests that the traditional hunt had now become of value for its own sake rather than as a means of counteracting a threat. In those days no self-respecting hunter would

Hunting the cowardly fox—Vale of Lune Hunt near Lancaster

lower himself to hunt the cowardly and witless fox. What brought about the need for this early attempt at conservation? Was it simply overhunting?

The incredible increase in the numbers of the aristocracy during Norman rule, and their need to excel in the hunt, no doubt contributed. The main cause of the wolf's extinction, however, was the reduction of the forests on which it relied for shelter. The regeneration of some woodland over which the King sported was more than cancelled out as the rapidly expanding monasteries built up great wealth based on one source of revenue — sheep, which grazed far and wide over the countryside. Thus the lamb may well have destroyed the wolf!

There will always be argument about the date of the last wolf hunt, usually depicted in folklore as a long-drawn-out chase and battle, ending with the human hero, his slaughtered dog close by, standing bloody but unbowed astride the last larger-than-life wolf. In England it has been suggested that Teesdale was the probable site and the date given is between 1485 and 1509, almost certainly during the reign of the first Tudor, the seventh Henry. However, the validity of this claim is questioned from at least two sources. It has been suggested that it

Some birds of the woodland edge have proved so adaptable that they have benefited from man's destruction of dense forest: (top) mistle thrush, (centre) blackbird, (bottom) chaffinch

would have been easier for the last remnants of the wolf population to escape the hunters by skulking in the extensive areas of marshland where hunting would be difficult if not impossible. Some writers have suggested that the district around Pickering in Yorkshire may have been the deathbed of England's last wolf. I have, however, a privately printed booklet called *The Last Wolf*, by Mrs Jerome Mercier, which suggests that the village of Cartmel in Cumbria was possibly the scene of the final hunt. Whatever the truth of the matter, the last wolf had vanished from England by 1530.

Scotland retained her woods longer than England, and hence wolf-hunting there went on with vigour throughout the sixteenth century. There is a graphic account of Mary, Queen of Scots, attending a hunt accompanied by a pack of hounds in the year 1563. It was not purely for fun either, since wolves were creating havoc in Sutherland, where they were reputed to have dug up corpses from churchyards during spells of bad weather. There is probably some truth in this, for Highlanders sought offshore islands, like Handa in Sutherland, for safe burial of their dead. Wolves were still rampant in the year 1577 during the reign of her son James VI (James I of England after the death of Elizabeth Tudor). If the price paid for a skin is a reasonable guide, wolves were scarce enough in Scotland by 1620, for in that year the sum of £6 13s 4d was paid for a single skin, a vast sum in those days. Again it was not hunting which brought about the end of the wolf there, but as in England the destruction of woodland habitat. Almost certainly the last wolf was extinct by 1700; a few argue that there is evidence a wolf was killed as late as 1848, but this is not generally accepted. The last wolf was killed in Ireland between the years 1766 and 1770.

The Plantagenets, feudal and in many ways insular monarchs, tried to preserve their forests, follow the hunt and keep the feudal laws. The Tudors were a different breed altogether. In the period from the defeat of Richard III at Bosworth Field, to the ascent — or perhaps more accurately descent — from Scotland of James Stuart, England was dragged, albeit willingly, into the industrial melting pot. Buildings mushroomed, bridges spanned rivers, the Navy was flexing its young muscles, and many more people were enjoying gracious living. Furniture was demanded and much was constructed of the finest timber, fires burned in grates, iron was smelted for farm machinery and weapons, glass was made in increasing quantity, and all these marks of civilisation demanded one basic raw material — wood. The Tudor energy crisis was real. Timber merchants desperately scoured the land in search of wood, giving a high priority to the good old English oak. Trees crashed to the ground, domestic pigs wintered in what was left of the forests and devoured vast quantities of acorns; the sheep thick on the uplands eagerly consumed any juicy saplings germinating from seeds dropped by such birds as jays and woodpigeons.

The fierce-fought Civil War of the 1640s generated an insatiable demand for timber, especially for gunpowder and iron smelting. Charles II, a much more intelligent monarch than is often allowed, set up the Royal Society and charged one of its members, John Evelyn, to investigate the state of the wildwoods of the kingdom which were now in such a state as to place the nation in acute danger. Evelyn did his work well; his *Sylva* was published in 1664, and one extract will suffice to highlight the problem and his suggested remedy.

> Since it is certain and demonstrable that all arts and artisans whosoever must fail and cease, if there were no timber and wood in a nation (for he that shall take his pen, and begin to set down what art mystery or trade belonging any way to human life, could be maintained and exercised without wood, will quickly find that I speak no paradox) I say, when all this be well considered, it will appear that we had better be without gold than without timber.

This was an influential publication produced at the instigation of a Stuart King, and it is not perhaps surprising to find that as early as 1609 the Scottish parliament passed legislation restricting the activities of iron foundries causing 'the utter wasting and consuming of the said [Pine] woods, which might be reserved for many better uses'. *Sylva* was certainly important and resulted in large-scale plantations. Whether these were intended for pleasure or profit matters not: for the first time in British history trees were being deliberately planted. It was merely a token gesture, however; consumption still far exceeded replacement. It was during this time that much of the English Lake District became an important industrial cog in the nation's machinery. Iron smelting needed wood charcoal, as did the manufacture of gunpowder. Charcoal burners scoured the woodlands, small blast furnaces sprang up almost overnight and functioned until the woodlands around them were exhausted. The workers then moved on, leaving the wreckage behind them, to ravage another area. The Scottish legislation was laid down very much with a view to curbing the activities of English smelters. Some respite was given to our woodlands by the discovery of a method of producing coke from coal and improving mining techniques for obtaining the latter though the metal industries realised its worth only slowly.

An inhabitant of Shakespeare's England would not recognise our present-day countryside. Most of their wide-open spaces have gone, hedged or fenced off into fields, in consequence of the Enclosure Acts of the eighteenth and nineteenth centuries. These Acts were a direct result of improved agricultural and animal-breeding techniques, developed under the pressure of an increasing population. Crops growing as fodder enabled farm cattle to be kept alive throughout the winter. They had to be fenced in, and wild herbivores and also predatory carnivores had to be fenced out. Fields were also needed to grow crops for human consumption. Pressure from land-owners resulted in the legislation that allowed them to fence in commons and open fields, often much to the detriment of the poorer people. Thus there evolved the enclosed farm such as we know today. Much of the uplands was not suitable for farming and here Evelyn's words were heeded and trees were planted with an eye to future profits. The enclosures obviously demanded hedges, and those with a head for business grew some timber trees as integral parts of these hedges.

Tree planting was thus accepted as a necessity and the devastated wildwoods began, albeit slowly, to be partially replaced. But the national economy was becoming far more complex. Factories began to produce goods for export and Britain's overseas trade boomed as never before or since. Quick and often immense profits could be made in a few short years. There was no incentive now for the wealthy to plough money into forestry, where the fruits of the financial outlay would only benefit their descendants. Moreover such timber as remained was eagerly consumed by nineteenth-century industry for building, pulp, pit props, telegraph poles and the sundry other needs of the new consumer society. Timber could now be imported from abroad, and in any case it was cheaper to do this. Britain's workers moved from villages into towns and all woodlands were used for was to provide cover for wildlife, which was shot by the wealthy in their many idle hours. Not until the Kaiser's war was it officially admitted again that Britain was woefully short of timber; it was as a direct result of this conflict that the Forestry Commission came into being. Based in London, it was initiated in 1916 when Asquith, the Prime Minister, appointed a committee 'to consider and report upon the best means of conserving and developing the woodland and forestry resources of the United Kingdom having regard to the experience gained during the war'.

The experience referred to was the wholesale destruction of broadleaved trees, a diminishing part of the English scene for centuries. The committee's solution was to set up the Forestry Commission, with the brief of planting millions of conifers which would grow a great deal more quickly than broadleaved ones. This policy was, and indeed still is, criticised on the grounds that a variety of trees provides better habitat for wildlife, that broadleaved woodlands are more suited to Britain's climate and soil types, and that a monoculture of conifers is aesthetically boring — arguments that were naturally shelved during World War II, a conflict that consumed vast areas of well-established timber, since that planted by the Commission was still far too immature to crop.

Since the early 1950s the Forestry Commission have realised that coniferous monocultures are relatively sterile as far as wildlife is concerned; a greater number of species is now planted, broadleaved trees being included, with a resultant economic and aesthetic improvement. There remains objection from naturalists in general and ornithologists in particular, to the Commission's still substantial new plantings of conifers; they complain that bird life is non-existent in coniferous woodland. This is an overstatement, but it does support fewer birds than the greener and lusher deciduous woodland with its greater variety of understorey plants and insect life.

When a historian was asked to state the effect of the French Revolution one hundred years after the event he drily remarked that it was too early to tell. It is also too early to judge the inter-relationship between a coniferous forest and the wildlife of Britain. How can we possibly state that wildlife will never adapt to these new forests which have been part of our country scene for less than half a century? Our natural fauna has been with us for much longer than this, and much more time is required for it to adapt to these new conditions. This is precisely why naturalists should observe these areas regularly and systematically. The Forestry Commission are also much more amenable to visitors than they used to be; they produce interesting booklets and many of their plantations are now open to the public.

One of the most notable of these is the forest of Grizedale, in Lakeland, where a well-organised Nature Trail is laid out. Whilst wandering around Grizedale on 18 October 1973, I was fortunate enough to see twenty-one buzzards in the air at the same time! The public relations are now of a high standard and a splendidly designed natural-history museum is open throughout the year. Not unnaturally the museum is biased towards deer, but the other mammals and birds are also represented. By prior appointment it is possible to hire a stilted hut which literally towers high above a forest clearing, and providing one is eager to rise early in the morning and able to climb the laddered framework to reach it, there is an ideal opportunity to watch red deer on their natural wanderings. (For those to whom interest in natural history is but one facet of a lively and enquiring mind, Grizedale offers a theatre in the forest which provides a varied programme of drama, music and poetry.)

If one has to select a date when the Forestry Commission woke up, then the year 1964 must be their Damascus Road. At that time the now-familiar picnic tables and benches in clearings did not exist; in 1969 there were 104 such sites and in 1974 the number was over 300.

In 1969 there were 92 forest trails, and by 1974 almost 400. Camping was encouraged and information centres, bird hides and observation hides sprouted like mushrooms. Man is now allowed back into his primitive environment and the outlook for our forests is brighter than it has been for thousands of years.

Many non-indigenous trees have been introduced to Britain in recent years, and one of the more important is the larch (*Larix decidua*), a deciduous conifer. (The word 'evergreen' is too often used as if it was synonymous with 'conifer'.) Its delicate spring greenery and golden autumnal dress make it a splendid sight almost throughout the year. The European larch was introduced from Central Europe at the beginning of the seventeenth century. It grows fast and is a very good pioneer tree. Its timber was once much in demand for the shipbuilding industry, being considered shot-proof. In the early days of the forestry industry the larch was very popular, but workers soon became disenchanted, as it proved to be so demanding of light that it could not be crowded — thought to be essential when land is expensive and profit margins vital. For these reasons foresters began to cultivate the Japanese larch (*Larix kaempferi*). This proved to be more adaptable and faster growing, but rather susceptible to disease. An experiment was therefore planned in the depths of the forest of Dunkeld in Perthshire at the commencement of the twentieth century. A female Japanese larch was pollinated from a European larch; the offspring were referred to as Dunkeld larches. These exhibit what biologists refer to as hybrid vigour, which is a crafty way of saying that the children are far more adaptable than either of their parents. It is these mongrel larches that are planted these days.

Because they are evergreen most conifers cast a heavy shade on the forest floor, which inhibits the growth of shrubs. Moreover many conifers are planted, indeed thrive, on acidic upland soils whose fertility is little enhanced by the durable needle-like leaves gradually shed from the branches. The larch, however, allows much more light to reach the ground, and its softer leaves are more easily decomposed, two characteristics which favour the development of a modest ground flora plus a community of insects and higher animals, such as herbivorous mammals, which depend on the plants for food and shelter. Other animals, such as insectivorous birds and carnivorous mammals, are in turn supported by these and a food chain is set up.

The fact that we are now planting woodlands which can support more elaborate systems of food chains is most encouraging. It is these food chains that are vital to our wildlife; it is because each link in a chain is so important that man's thoughtless interference, or more positively his choice of trees to plant, for example, becomes a serious matter.

Larch

The Food Chain

The sun, a medium-sized star, pours out a continual stream of energy. Some radiated energy falls on each of its nine orbiting planets, including the one called earth. The key to life on our planet involves the trapping of this solar energy, and using it to power a chemical reaction to convert simple raw materials into food. The simple raw materials are water and carbon dioxide and the food produced is called glucose. This reaction can occur anywhere on earth where water and carbon dioxide exist and the sun is shining, not only within the body of a plant. It does however proceed so slowly that it would not be of any practical use to the plant. What is needed is a chemical, a catalyst, which really acts as an accelerator to speed up the reaction. Just such a chemical, chlorophyll, has been evolved by plants for this purpose, and its colour is the most consistent attribute of green plants. This is why only green plants are able to generate a supply of energy-rich food by the process of photosynthesis (*photos*, light, *synthesis*, building up). Thus to return to our food chain we have plants as the first link, the primary producers.

Feeding upon these primary producers are herbivorous animals or primary consumers; included here would be earthworms, insects, snails, deer, rabbits, voles and so on. Some animals have taken the food chain one link further and are referred to either as secondary consumers or as carnivores: included here are the small insect-eating birds such as the robin, the tits or the dunnock. Finally we have the top carnivores, often referred to as tertiary consumers: these include the beasts and birds of prey, such as foxes and weasels, owls and hawks.

To complete the picture, when the top carnivore dies its body decays by the action of bacteria, carbon dioxide returns to the atmosphere and other chemicals are returned to the soil; nothing is wasted.

The concept of the food chain is an important one, but it will soon be realised that it is very much an over-simplification. Many plants (primary producers) are fed upon by a variety of herbivores (primary consumers), all of which eat not one plant species but several. The herbivores in turn are eaten by the carnivores (secondary and tertiary consumers) and they do not usually confine themselves to just one prey species. The long-eared owl of a conifer wood, for example, will eat voles, mice, several species of small bird and even insects. By remaining flexible in its choice of prey the owl protects itself against shortage of any one item, and so improves its own survival chances in an environment where the choices are often limited. Thus rather than a series of simple food chains we have a complex food web. The food chain and food web concepts, however, give no idea of the relative populations of producers and consumers. It is obvious that any predator which becomes more numerous than its prey is doomed. This logical relationship is expressed very well as a food pyramid. The top carnivores, few in number, appear at the apex, and the primary producers, in bulk, at the base.

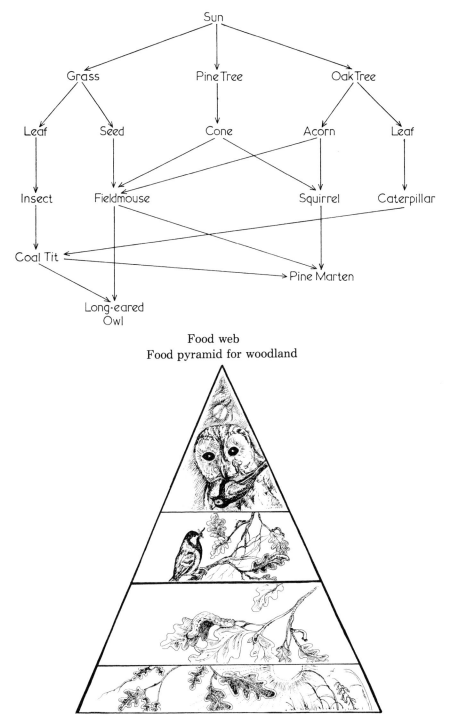

Food web
Food pyramid for woodland

These pyramids allow us to see in clear relief the imbalances of the past. A classic case was the demise of the deer on the Karbab Plateau in Arizona, USA, early this century. When man removed its natural predators — pumas and wolves — deer numbers increased 25-fold. In two winters the deer had eaten themselves out of house and home and the population crashed from about 100,000 to 10,000; the sorely depleted habitat and the predators were slow to recover and redress the balance normally maintained by the reaction between predator and prey. It is interesting to consider the effect of the extinction of the wolf and the reduction in predators such as polecats and pine martens upon the woodland food pyramids.

Once the principles here are understood it should be less difficult to prevent repetitions which, with the human populations higher than ever and still rising, could be irreparable. Mankind, at least in the Western world, must obviously be considered as a tertiary consumer, and any disruption of our food chains, webs and pyramids, at whatever linkage, will be quickly and painfully felt.

A good example of 'pre-ecological' thinking was the setting up in developing coniferous forests of large numbers of nest boxes to attract breeding birds, titmice in particular. In a monoculture of introduced conifers there will be a shortage of indigenous insects; and it is their larvae that form the staple diet of young birds. Obviously large numbers of nest boxes encouraged more birds than could be supported by the existing food supply and the food pyramid was bound to be disrupted. Two things however, have prevented total disaster. Firstly there is the resilience of the birds themselves. Great tits in boxes in Scots pine (Breckland) lost about 38 per cent of their fledglings, a higher figure than losses in deciduous woodlands — in such a wood at Wytham, Oxfordshire, this figure is below 10 per cent. Scots pine is however an indigenous species and the losses in woods dominated by 'foreign species' may be quite a lot higher. The birds in coniferous woods, however, may combat these losses by extending their breeding season and producing a second brood. The Commission are now varying the species planted, and even including some native deciduous trees, usually around the edges of plantations, and this obviously increases the insect populations, thus allowing a greater survival rate among the insect-eating birds.

The main crop nowadays is the Norway spruce (*Picea abies*), known in Britain as the Christmas tree. It is not native to Britain, but became a popular part of our Christmas rituals during the life of Queen Victoria's husband, Albert, who imported the tradition from his native Germany. Unlike the larch, the spruce is evergreen and produces a heavy shade; the attraction of spruce plantations for wildlife will be limited, especially where the trees are of uniform age and size, though bird life is not totally absent there. I have found the dominant bird in these areas to be the woodpigeon, with chaffinches, coal tits, goldcrests and wrens also present. The odd heronry is found in spruce forests and even linnets and yellowhammers have bred, especially when the plantations are in their infancy. These seedling forests are also popular breeding sites for that splendid bird the short-eared owl.

The Commission have recently taken a significant step by funding a census of all trees, a mammoth task, to be completed in 1982. Modern technology will be used, including extensive aerial photography, but a great deal of foot slogging will also be required. Even isolated trees, and those in towns, will be counted and some attempt will be made to estimate age, life expectancy and the volume of timber contained. It is obvious that the woodlands of Britain have reached a very low ebb — again — but at least it is now realised that something must be done and our grandchildren will have more trees to enjoy than we have had.

Nor is it only our wildlife and our own aesthetic sense that demand more trees. We still need vast quantities of timber for industry, and although specific uses will almost certainly change, the demand for the raw material will not slacken. Wood may even be required to play its part in combating future energy crises. In Sweden it is reckoned that most of the nation's energy needs can be met by planting tracts of fast-growing willows and harvesting them to burn — either in the form of powdered wood or as oil extracted from it. The demand for paper, too, is accelerating all the time. At last Britain is planting a crop of her own instead of importing from other lands whose own supply is not inexhaustible.

Thus this chapter can be concluded on a note of cautious optimism and we can go on to discuss the fabric of the woodlands we have today and the wildlife therein.

2
The Woodland Web

Little now remains of our once extensive natural forest cover, and even what we have has been so drastically altered that it can hardly be referred to as natural. When we consider how a woodland develops from barren ground or even directly from the bed-rock, we are tracing in an evolutionary sense the succession which culminated in the formation of ancient woodlands; and part of the same path is followed on a smaller time scale whenever a wood regenerates from the site of a devastated area.

Our present-day woodlands are usually dominated by one or perhaps two species of tree; birch, ash, oak, beech and pine woods each have their own characteristic flora and fauna, though of course some ecological features are common to all woodlands.

Initially the earth was devoid of vegetation. The gradual cooling of the bare rock over centuries, and the more immediate effect of hot day-time and cold night-time temperatures, caused uneven expansion and contraction in the many different forms of rock. Such cracks in time fill with rain water, and on its journey from heavy cloud to thirsty earth the water picks up sufficient carbon dioxide to form a dilute solution of carbonic acid. The immediate effect is perhaps minimal, but any potholer will tell you that the solvent effect of rain water acting over millions of years looks nothing short of miraculous, and that if St Paul's Cathedral was dropped into many of these caverns it would disappear. Further pressure on the cracks in rocks, already widened and deepened by solvent action, occurs when the water within them freezes, since 10 cubic centimetres of water will form 11 cubic centimetres of ice. Just as frozen water may burst metal pipes, so it tends to fragment rocks. Gradually, then, the rock becomes powdered and the particles are blown along the ground until meeting either an obstruction or depression, when a pile of powdered mineral accumulates.

On this food-deficient substrate only one form of life can survive: this is called lichen, which is often written off as just another simple

Male redstart

plant. In fact it is neither simple nor just one plant, but a combination of two plants which live together for the mutual benefit of each other — a happy arrangement known as symbiosis. One partner is a type of fungus which provides the anchorage to the substrate, and it is thought to produce an acid which is capable of dissolving rock. It cannot, however, make food. This deficiency is made good by its partner, a green alga. This makes food by the process of photosynthesis. The algae multiply within the fungus and some cells will die and become available to the fungus as food. There are many many types of lichen which are often ignored by naturalists or dismissed as 'stains' or marks on walls or tree-trunks. They are, however, of great significance to life in the latter half of the twentieth century, since they are very susceptible to atmospheric pollution, notably by sulphur dioxide, and can therefore be monitored and used as pollution indicators. If lichens are disappearing, then the environment must be deteriorating, and if the lichen population is increasing, in numbers of species and also of individuals, then a corresponding decrease in atmospheric pollution must be occurring.

A variety of animals put lichens to more fundamental use: insects find a niche within the body of the lichens and are hunted by such birds as wheatears, redstarts and pied wagtails, which can often be seen picking their way along the encrusted walls of country districts. Other birds such as the long-tailed tit and the chaffinch use them in nest construction; they give substance to the nest and also provide camouflage.

31

Female redstart

   In time lichens perish and their decaying bodies provide nutrients,
which when mixed with the powdered rock particles form soil. This is
best considered as a dynamic substance full of life forms, the decaying
remains of forms which have died, with water, air and mineral
particles. Providing the soil is damp, other plant types, better suited
to the conditions created by the lichens, can now grow and thrive. For
example liverworts and mosses (together called bryophytes) and the
ferns (pteridophytes) thrive under these conditions. Eventually these
are overshadowed and replaced by low herbs, which may in turn be
followed by a shrub layer. As these flourish and die they add more
nutrients to the system and with this extra humus the soil has now
deepened to such an extent that we may now contemplate the survival
of deeper-rooted trees. The first trees to grow are called pioneer
species. These need open space and plenty of light. Their leaves fall to
the ground, adding more humus to the soil and increasing its depth.
The shade provided ameliorates the climate, tending to conserve heat
generated within the community and at the same time shielding the
centre from the shrivelling rays of the summer sun.

Long-tailed tit and nest

Gradually the pioneer species are succeeded by other trees which require the deep soil produced by the hardier settlers. These latter species shade out the pioneers and in time the whole area may be dominated by one or perhaps two species. Thus on heather moors, pioneering birches may eventually be dominated by pines. The total process is called succession and the final association of trees is called the climax vegetation. Much of Britain's woodlands if left alone would have an oak climax. Very often, however, the climax vegetation is not determined by nature but, as already described, by man's deliberate and often disastrous interference.

A careful look at a natural wood will reveal four clearly defined levels: the ground layer, the field layer, the shrub layer and finally the tree layer. Any scientific survey of a wood will have separate species lists for each layer and it will be found that not only the plants are associated with a particular level, but also the animals, including the birds.

33

Tree layer ↑

Shrub layer

Field layer

Ground layer

34

The Ground Layer

This layer is dominated by mosses and liverworts, particularly in damp woodlands. The woods situated on the western side of Britain therefore tend to be richer in mosses than those on the eastern side. Mosses and liverworts are not always popular with the amateur naturalists and plant spotters: so few species have simple English names and learning over 500 names as complex as *Eurynchium striatum* or *Fissidens taxifolius* can be somewhat of a baptism of fire. However, becoming familiar with the common species is not too difficult.

As you might expect the mineral composition of the woodland soil plays a vital role in determining which species grow in a particular place.

The Field Layer

This layer is probably the most familiar to the average country lover or even naturalist, since the flowers which dominate it are often brightly coloured and heavily perfumed. The list of species is extensive and obviously varies from place to place; but typical, at least in mature deciduous woodland, are primrose, wood anemone, the delightful little green-flowered moschatel, herb robert, dog's mercury, bugle and the strong-smelling wild garlic. Some species tend to be associated with woodlands dominated by one species of tree. Moschatel, for example, shows a distinct liking for ashwoods, the white helleborine for beech, twinflower (*Linnaea borealis*) for pinewoods, whilst birchwoods are so deficient in nitrates that they are more noted for their fungi than for their flowers. Most of the inhabitants of the field layer are obliged to flower very early in the year: growing plants must have light, and once the leaves have appeared on the larger trees, little light can penetrate the canopy and reach the woodland floor. This pre-vernal (before-spring) growth of flowers is one of the most delightful periods in the calendar of our British woodlands.

The Shrub Layer

This layer is more difficult to define, since no strictly scientific distinction can be made between a shrub and a tree. One useful point of contrast is that a mature shrub usually puts out branches almost from ground level, whereas a mature tree usually has a couple of metres of fairly straight trunk before putting out branches. Common members of the shrub layer include blackthorn (sloe), whitethorn (hawthorn), elder and holly, but the dominant species in British woodlands is hazel.

The four layers of woodland vegetation

In some heavily grazed woods, or in those like beech or pine woods which cast a very heavy shade, the shrub layer can be greatly diminished, or in extreme cases lacking altogether. In most woods, however, the shrub layer is quite dense and provides both invertebrates and vertebrates with cover, food and breeding habitat.

The Tree Layer

Obviously the taller species of tree will dominate this area and shade out any competitors including weaker or younger members of their own species. The final natural succession will be determined by a number of factors, including soil, slope and climate. Thus in some areas pine will dominate, ash in others and in yet others the mighty oak will hold sway. The climax species obviously determines the extent of the shrub layer, which in turn will affect the field layer, and so on down to the ground layer. So we should know the various types of climax woodland found in Britain and the plants and animals dependent upon each.

Birch Woods

There are two species of birch native to these islands, the silver birch (*Betula pendula*) and the downy birch (*Betula pubescens*). A third, the dwarf birch (*Betula nana*), never forms woodlands and is a distinctly northern species. The two main species, especially the downy birch, are very resistant to frost and this makes the birch a very important pioneer plant. It provides protection to longer-living trees during their juvenile stages, and is then ungratefully shaded out by them as they mature. Birch woods survive in areas where the climate is too severe for other species. In Scotland and in some parts of Northern England there are splendid birch woods in existence, and these constitute the climax of the vegetational succession in these areas. In Greenland, for example, birch is the only native tree: the species appears to diminish in size as you move from south to north, a phenomenon which is hardly surprising.

The two species are easily distinguishable. The silver birch has not only a light silvery-coloured bark, but its branches almost always droop at the tips (*pendula*—hanging). The twigs of silver birch are covered by pale wart-like bumps, a feature which is not seen in the downy birch. The twigs of the latter are often covered with hairs (*pubescens*—downy). There are also differences in leaf shape: those of

Wood anemone

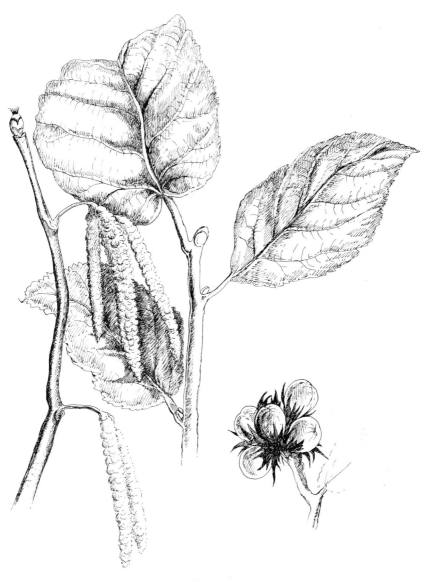

Hazel

the silver birch are more pointed and the toothed margins are much deeper than those of the downy birch.

In the past man made much use of the birch. As was usual in the days of true woodcraft, little if anything at all was wasted. A yellow dye was made from the leaves. The timber was used in the preparation of excellent charcoal, used in the manufacture of gunpowder and

Dog's mercury

crayons. Birch was apparently first choice for these purposes even when other timbers were available, and in some northern areas other species were in any case scarce or non-existent. In the Highlands of Scotland, for example, almost the whole economy was based upon birch. Houses, furniture, carts, gates, fences, ploughs, harrows and even rope were fashioned from it. Its branches were burned as fuel to warm houses, distil whisky, smoke herring and cure ham. Youngsters were chastised with it, roofs thatched with it, and it was strewn as a bed for tired bodies to rest upon. In parts of Northern Europe great tracts of birch have been killed by the excessive tapping of sap from the trunks to make birch wine. The birch also has considerable aesthetic appeal:

> ... most beautiful
> Of forest trees, the lady of the Woods.

The beautiful lady can be greedy and Madam Birch's long roots spread far and wide rather than deep, and thus she is able to survive in areas which offer few nutrients. This does mean that in a birch wood individual trees tend to be widely spaced. Because the ground which supports them is not rich in minerals the list of flowers found in birch woods tends to be disappointingly short. This is especially true of upland areas. Occasionally a lowland birch wood may support a substantial shrub layer, almost always dominated by hazel, and a field layer consisting of wood anemone and pignut. The ground layer consists of several species of mosses and liverworts − bryophytes.

The botanist, however, can appreciate that some of Britain's most attractive fungi thrive in birch woods. One of the best known is the highly poisonous but not deadly fly agaric (*Amanita muscaria*), easily recognised by its scarlet cap covered with white or cream warty spots. The best time to look for fungi is during the autumn months. This is because it is only during the reproductive season that the fruiting bodies − the parts we recognise − appear above ground. All these structures are merely bags of spores lifted clear of the ground so that they may be launched into the wind, by which agency they are largely spread. The main long-living portion of the fungal body consists of spreading strands called hyphae; together these are termed the mycelium.

Fungi never possess chlorophyll and therefore they are unable to manufacture their own food from basic raw materials. For this reason some biologists choose to classify fungi as a third kingdom, belonging to neither Animals nor Plants.

Since they are unable to photosynthesise, fungi must obtain their

Birch wood (previous page)—Ightenhill woods, Burnley

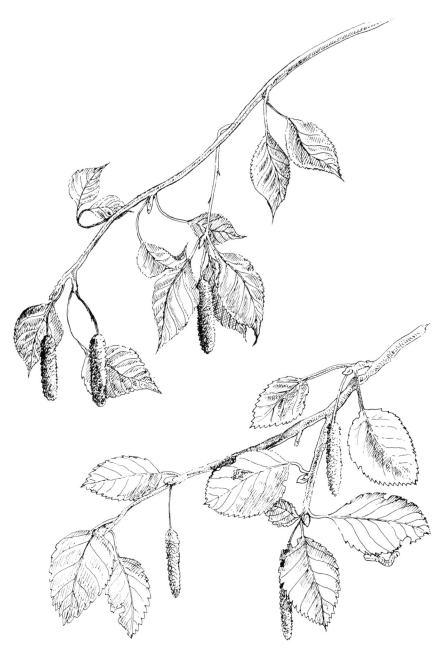

Twigs and leaves of silver birch (above) and downy birch (below)

Fly agaric

sustenance by other means. They may produce digestive juices and secrete them out of the mycelium into the soil. These fluids digest the dead, decaying remains of organisms and the 'soup' so produced is absorbed by the fungal body. This is called saprophytic feeding, and many species, including the fly agaric, adopt it to tap the great store of debris on the woodland floor. Some fungi enter into a symbiotic partnership with a green plant, notably trees but also some flowering plants, including some remarkable associations with orchids. The hyphae usually penetrate the cells of the plant root and the fungus is able to avail itself of the food material contained therein. In exchange the fungus seems able to concentrate such mineral salts as are available in the poor soil and thus make them more available to the green plant. This intimate and often mutually essential relationship between the two partners is called mycorrhiza. So important is this

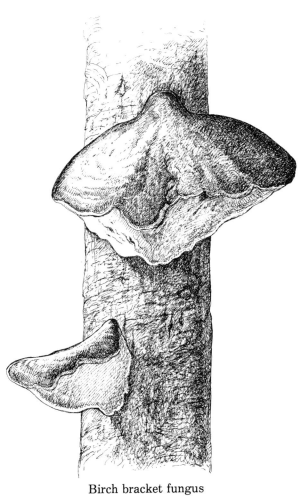

Birch bracket fungus

association that in commercial forestry new saplings may be artificially infected with the appropriate fungus before planting.

The only other nutritional option open to the higher fungi is to attach themselves directly to the body of another living organism and take all their food material from the host. Such fungi are out-and-out parasites and many are found associated with birch. The best-known example is the birch bracket fungus (*Piptoporus betulinus*). It is usually greyish in colour, darker on the top than beneath, and looks very much like an athlete's discus protruding from the tree. Its mycelium is situated deep in the tissues of its host, and its hyphae penetrate the cells and suck out the food-rich juices. The vulnerability of birch to fungal attack makes it quite attractive to hole-nesting birds, especially the great spotted woodpecker (*Dendrocopus major*) which can easily chisel out cavities in the portions of trunk rotted by fungi. Following fungal attack the soft tissues of the tree become rich in insect larvae feeding upon the decaying wood, and thus the woodpeckers also have invertebrate food close by.

Prominent among the larvae found are those of moths. A well-known lepidopterist once told me that she did not find birch woods particularly fruitful: I was surprised, since over 130 moth species have been identified in birch woods. They can be captured by 'sugaring' (painting tree trunks with a solution attractive to moths, made up variously of molasses, brown sugar, rum or beer), or by the use of an ultra-violet light. One species frequently captured during summer is probably the most documented insect in the world, the peppered moth (*Biston betularia*). It holds the distinction of demonstrating more forcibly than any other species the force of evolution in action, by exhibiting what has become known as 'industrial melanism'. Of the many ways in which Britain's countryside was altered by the events of the Industrial Revolution, perhaps the most striking was the increase in atmospheric pollution, as soot from burning coal spewed upwards from domestic and industrial premises and was spread by the wind. Extensive work by many scientists, E. B. Ford and H. B. D. Kettlewell in particular, on the peppered moth has been exciting. Before the Industrial Revolution the moth was white with black speckling on the wings and body — hence its vernacular name of pepper-and-salt moth. This has been called the typical form. In 1847 a black variety of the species was caught near Manchester and has been called *carbonaria*. Regular monitoring since this time has shown that *carbonaria* has become more common in industrial areas whilst the typical form holds its own in unpolluted country areas.

Briefly the explanation is as follows. If equal numbers of the lighter typical form and the dark *carbonaria* form are released in an industrial area they will seek shelter on the trunks of trees. In sooty atmospheres *carbonaria* will be less obvious to predators than the typical form, and so more of the typical form will be eaten. This will obviously lead to *carbonaria* becoming the commoner form. In country areas the reverse will hold; *carbonaria* will stand out against the cleaner trunks and the typical form will survive better. In our era of Clean Air Acts we shall probably see a reversal of a trend which has been dominant for over 100 years, and the typical form should find its habitat improving; this underlines nature's adaptability.

The caterpillar of the peppered moth feeds on a variety of plants including rose, bramble, elm and oak, but birch is probably its most frequent food. If you look for it, you will find a great deal of variation in its colour, but greenish-brown is the basic shade and the last

Industrial melanism in the peppered moth

segment of the abdomen is tinged with purple and bears two points. A nocturnal feeder, if disturbed it will fall to the ground and behave as if it was dead. These caterpillars are active from July to September and in September change into black, shiny pupae which can be found at the base of trees. The adult moths emerge in April and May and can be found on the wing up to the end of July.

Ash Woods

The ash (*Fraxinus excelsior*) is a relative of the lilac and the privet and a member of the olive family. It is not good at surviving extremes of hot or cold and therefore thrives best in temperate areas of Europe. Even so, it is a fairly hardy species, and can be found flourishing high up hillsides, especially in limestone areas of Britain. The delightful ash has been a central figure in the folklore of many cultures. The Ancient Greeks knew it well and called it *Melea*. It was used for the handles of their spears and Cupid was alleged to have used it for the shafts of his arrows. The Romans named it *Fraxinus* and their great natural historian Pliny had plenty to say about it, although he does take considerable poetic licence: he claimed that snakes would not shelter beneath its branches, and would sooner creep into a fire than squirm beneath the ash. Dioscorides, a physician, carried this belief one step further by recommending the juice of the ash as an antidote for snake-bite.

It is in Teutonic mythology, however, that the ash reaches the height of its fame. Here indeed was the 'Tree of Life'. An enormous ash tree filled space — its roots descended into the underworld, its crown touched heaven, its enormous branches supported our world. Perched on the crown was a majestic eagle who superintended events below. In this small task he was ably assisted by a squirrel, which could climb up and down the tree with sufficient dexterity to carry essential messages. Man's religion was tightly bound up with the lore of the forest which clothes his earth. In more recent times too the ash has been a part of the beliefs of mankind. Gilbert White in his *Natural History of Selborne*, written towards the close of the eighteenth century, relates one story.

> In a farmyard near the middle of this village stands at this day a row of pollard-ashes, which, by the seams and long cicatrices down their sides, manifestly show that in former times they have been cleft assunder. These trees, when young and flexible, were severed and held open by wedges, while ruptured children, stripped naked, were pushed through the apertures, under a persuasion that by such a process the poor babes would be cured of their infirmity. As soon as the operation was over, the tree, in the suffering part, was plastered with loam and carefully swathed up. If the parts were coalesced and soldered together, as usually fell out, where the feat was performed with any adroitness at all, the party was cured;

Shrew

but where the cleft continued to gape, the operation, it was supposed, would prove ineffectual. Having occasion to enlarge my garden not long since, I cut down two or three such trees, one of which did not grow together. We have several persons now living in the village, who in their childhood, were supposed to be healed by this superstitious ceremony, derived down, perhaps, from our saxon ancestors who practiced it before their conversion to Christianity.

Ashwoods are known to be rich in small mammals. The common shrew is an example, and this creature was intimately bound up in ash folklore. To quote Gilbert White again,

At the south corner of the Plestor, or area near the church, there stood, about twenty years ago, a very old, grotesque, hollow pollard-ash which for ages had been looked on with no small veneration as a shrew-ash. Now a shrew-ash is an ash whose twigs or branches, when gently applied to the limbs of cattle, will immediately relieve the pains which a beast suffers from the running of a shrew mouse over the part affected; for it is supposed that a shrew mouse is of so baneful and deleterious a nature that wherever it creeps over a beast, be it horse, cow or sheep, the suffering animal is afflicted with cruel anguish and threatened with the loss of the use of the limb. Against this accident, to which they were continually liable, our provident forefathers always kept a shrew-ash at hand, which, when once medicated would maintain its virtue for ever.

The English name of ash is derived from the Saxon word *aesc* − not from the 'ashy' colour of the bark. In winter the grey bark and large flattened black buds make the ash one of the easier trees for our children to recognise, and in summer its large pinnate leaves are distinctive: each leaf usually has a terminal leaflet with five pairs of leaflets behind it, the whole supported on a stout twig. The leaves appear very late in the season, often a month or more after the purple flowers have bloomed. These flowers seem to be one of the favourite foods of the woodpigeon, which often displays amazing dexterity in balancing to reach them — similar to its skilful performances in autumn when it gorges itself on elderberry. In late summer and autumn the fruits of the ash hang from the branches, each ash key as it is called consisting of a single seed with a winged extension to enable it to spin along in the autumn winds. At first the keys are fresh green and succulent, and if gathered before they go dry and brown they can be pickled as a pleasant addition to a salad.

The ash has a long and distinguished history as timber. Its resilience has been turned to use in the handles of hammers, axes, spears and police truncheons, while its pliability, especially when young, renders it useful in the manufacture of walking sticks and hoops for barrels. Even the bark was put to good use: before cheap paper was developed, the outer bark was stripped from the tree and written upon.

Ash, as we have seen, comes into leaf late and with lots of light thus able to reach the ground in spring, the layering in an ash wood can be most impressive. Though ash can form a wood in its own right, it frequently shares dominance with oak. Since oak also comes into leaf late, the field and shrub layers in these mixed woodlands is perhaps the richest of any in Britain. Thus we have a contrast to the rather bare aspect of birch woods and a most valuable habitat.

The ground layer has a selection of moss species, but it is in the field layer that richness really reveals itself. The observant naturalist should have no difficulty in identifying many species, including moschatel, dog's mercury, nettle-leaved bellflower, red campion, birds-eye, speedwell and wood anemone. Ash woods tend to thrive particularly well on lime-rich soils and so, in addition to the normal shrub layer of hazel and field maple, you may find dogwood, guelder rose (in the south of England you may also get the wayfaring tree), privet, hawthorn, blackthorn, elder and bird cherry. Old man's beard may also be found tangling over the shrubs, again mostly in southern England.

Ash is not particularly notable for its attractiveness to insects — under 40 species are on the list for ash woods, whereas birch woods are known to harbour 140 species. Within the trunk of the ash, however, is played out one of the most impressive melodramas in nature's repertoire. Sometimes you can find a goat moth (*Cossus cossus*) resting upon a tree trunk, usually during June, July and August — light brown in colour, the segments on the abdomen etched with darker brown, with a black U-shape on the thorax and an orange-brown head. It is not the adults, however, that are most likely to be encountered, but the brownish-pink caterpillars. These have a distinct smell of billy-goat which lends them their vernacular name. A goat-moth caterpillar does not consume leaves but has mouth parts and digestive juices adapted for spending some three or four years

Ash: A bud, B keys, C leaves, D flower

burrowing its way through the timber just below the bark. Knowing how rapidly caterpillars of most moths and butterflies develop into adults, we may well ask why the goat moth's larval development is so slow. It turns out to be geared to the difficulty of extracting sufficient nutriment from the diet of wood, which the caterpillar is obliged to chew up in vast quantities. Raised on a diet of beetroot the larvae will mature and pupate in a year! When the caterpillar eventually pupates it will leave tell-tale holes in the trunk. Goat moths eat ash, and they also occur on elm, birch, popular and willow. The smell of goats, or perhaps simply the excavation work, is not unnoticed by other insects; various beetles and large numbers of red admiral butterflies can often be seen investigating holes made by the goat moth, attracted to the sugary sap exuded through them by the tree.

Another much more sinister visitor to the abode of the goat-moth caterpillar is *Lampronata setosa*, one species of ichneumon fly. Ichneumons belong to the Hymenoptera, a group of insects which includes bees, wasps and ants. The female ichneumon skulks around the tree trunks, her senses highly primed, and she can detect the presence of a goat moth, even though it may be below the bark, having eaten its way in from the entrance hole. The ichneumon has a long, flexible laying tube, the ovipositor, which she works rather like a gimlet to bore into the bark and then into the body of the caterpillar. Then she passes her eggs down the tube and lodges them in her victim. They hatch inside the body of the caterpillar and literally eat the poor thing alive. Nature may be red in tooth and claw in the jungles of Africa, Asia and South America, but deep in a British ash wood some of the necessary links in the food chain are grisly enough.

Oak Woods

Such is the magnificence of a British oak wood that a book could well be devoted solely to a description of its ecology and its importance to our wildlife; a second volume could be written on its historical associations.

Oak woodland left to its own devices would be the climax vegetation in this country in many places, and it is here that we approach the perfect demonstration of layering. The ground layer is very rich in mosses, both as regards diversity and abundance; commonly found examples are *Fissidens taxifolius* and *Thamnium alopecurum.* The field layer is lush, and prominent among the flowers are early purple orchis, wood anemone, enchanter's nightshade, ground ivy, primrose and dog's mercury — often the dominant flower of this layer. Probably because it has green rather insignificant flowers, the dog's mercury tends to be overlooked and it is the primrose which catches the eye of the poet — as in John Clare's sonnet written in 1816.

> Welcome pale primrose. Starting up between
> Dead matted leaves of ash and oak, that strew
> The every lawn, the wood and spinney through,
> Mid creeping moss and ivy's darker green.

Primroses bloom during late March, April and May throughout the

Primrose

British Isles and are particularly common on the western side. I remember the thrill of finding a primrose in flower in a Lakeland oak—ash wood on New Year's Day. It has a great variety of vernacular names to add to its rather ugly scientific name, *Primula vulgaris*, such as lent rose or butter rose, and my own personal favourite, 'the darling of April'. The species is much less common than it used to be because the sweet-smelling blooms have been over-picked, which is perhaps understandable; what cannot be excused is the selfish habit of digging up whole plants from the unplanned woodlands and replanting them in man's regimented gardens. Fortunately a wild flower protection Act, and persistent publicity about the flower's plight, seem to be taking effect, at least to some degree, and so once again the conservationist has hopes.

If a primrose flower is examined closely it can be seen to consist not of separate petals, but of a tube made up of five petals joined together; the top edges of the petals are notched. And there are two distinct

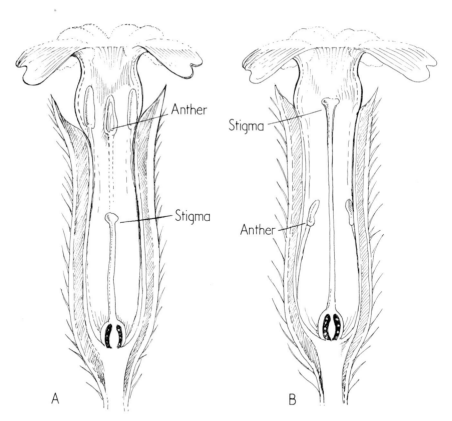

The two types of primrose: A thrum-eyed and B pin-eyed

types of flower, though each plant bears only one sort: pin-eyed and thrum-eyed. Both are true primroses but in the pin-eyed sort the stigma sticks out at the top of the flower like a pin-head. The stigma is joined to the ovary by a long tube, the style, and this is the female portion of the flower. The stamens, the male parts, are positioned halfway up the flower, well below the level of the stigma. In the thrum-eyed primrose these positions are reversed. This arrangement helps to ensure that the pollen produced in the stamens of an individual flower is not deposited on the stigma of the same flower. Too much self-pollination tends to weaken the genetic vigour of the plant's descendants.

Bees, attracted both by the bright colour and the perfume, visit primroses for the nectar produced at the base of the petals. If a bee visits a pin-eyed primrose it pokes its long tongue into the flower to get at the nectar. The front of its head this time rests on the stamens and gets dusted with pollen. The tongue pushes down in search of nectar and in so doing touches the stigma. Some of the pollen taken previously from the thrum-eyed flower is dusted on to the sticky stigma. There are approximately equal numbers of pin-eyed and thrum-eyed flowers, and by the law of averages the third flower to be visited will be another pin-eyed flower. The front of the bee's head will touch the stigma and a proportion of the pollen will be transferred from insect to flower. Thus both pin-eyed and thrum-eyed flowers are pollinated. This phenomenon, discovered by Charles Darwin and called heterostyly, has another remarkable aspect: the pollen grains of the thrum-eyed flowers are coarser than those of the pin-eyed flowers and, like lock and key, each fits best into the stigma of the other flower type and is more readily accepted by it. This again helps to encourage cross-fertilisation. If the pollen grain was deposited on the stigma of a flower of a different species it would probably not develop (although the primrose does hybridise with the cowslip, a close relative, to produce the 'false oxlip'). The stigma of each species produces a sugary solution of a precise strength, each species having its own individual concentration. The solution stimulates the pollen grain to develop a tube which penetrates the stigma and grows all the way down through the style into the ovary. The male cell within the tube is carried along and eventually joins with the female cell in the ovary, producing a fertile seed.

As the delicate aroma of the primrose fades from the oak wood it is replaced by the heady scent wafted by the breeze playing over the carpets of bluebells. This beautiful flower too has many vernacular names, including adder flower, crow flower, crow foot, crow legs and crow toes, bummock and, even more comical, grammer greylegs, granfer griggles and granfer griggle sticks. Perhaps the most meaningful of them all is 'pride of the wood'; it has also been called the wild hyacinth, though it actually belongs to the lily family; its old scientific name was *Hyacinthus non-scriptus*. On the petals of members of the true hyacinth family you will discover 'writing'; you may even be able to detect the initials AL. Their absence on the bluebell explains its name, *non scriptus*. When it was finally accepted that the bluebell was not a hyacinth, its scientific name was changed to *Endymion non-scriptus*.

The plant grows from an underground bulb which provides the food enabling the flower to grow during the months of May and June. Once the new growth has begun the leaves manufacture food and much of this is passed down the stem to form next year's bulb. Beneath the leaf litter and soil the bulb lives on, safe from winter frost, after the rest of the plant has withered away. To pick the flowers is a pity nowadays, but it is far more damaging to take the bulbs. Continued for just a few years the plundering of bulbs could reduce the bluebell, which looks so magnificent in large sweeps, to just a few unimpressive blooms. This has already happened to another member of the lily family,

Convallaria majalis, better known to country folk as lily-of-the-valley.

Each bluebell bulb sends up a number of narrow leaves each about half a metre (20 inches or so) tall. The stems are soft and juicy, and as the flowers, each with three sepals and petals, hang on one side of it only, it bends under their combined weight. After pollination and fertilisation, black seeds are produced. Thus the bluebell can reproduce vegetatively, from the bulbs, or sexually from seeds.

Our wood-dwelling ancestors may have waxed poetic about the glories of a bluebell wood, but they also knew some uses for their flowers, and both primrose and bluebell were functional as well as decorative. In the New Forest, for example, the workmen boiled up primrose flowers with fat which they used to treat cuts and abrasions, whilst their children were told to chew the flowers if they wished to see fairies. Primroses were worn as a protection against witches and in the Isle of Man, where occult traditions were strong, cowsheds were decorated with primroses on May Day to keep evil at bay. Bluebells were put to an even more practical use: in the Middle Ages their sap was boiled into a glue by fletchers for fixing feathers into the shafts of arrows.

The field layer is a great deal richer around the edge of the oak wood than in the dark, cool centre. Thus man's activities have had some beneficial effect on wildlife by breaking up the dense forests and letting in light. Also, because the woodland edge is a meeting place for the flora and fauna of both open country and forest, it supports a great diversity of wildlife. Many butterflies find the right combination of sunlight and food plants here: for example the leaves of violets are fed upon by the caterpillars of lovely fritillary butterflies. Especially in the south of the country, fritillary species are found in oak woodlands — the silver-washed, pearl-bordered, small-bordered and high brown. In clearings, large patches of stinging nettles can flourish, and their leaves are devoured by the caterpillars of the small tortoiseshell butterfly. In summer, therefore, oak woods contain an abundance of caterpillars in the field layer, and the food chain is completed by small birds such as wrens and robins, which feed both themselves and their developing young to a great extent on caterpillar prey. In turn, predators like the tawny owl wait for dusk to crush any unwary little bird and feed it to their own hungry families. Most small birds only live for a year or two, but we rarely find those that die of 'natural causes' lying on the woodland floor, so rapidly are they consumed by scavengers and bacteria. The waste not, want not, policy of the natural economy carries through.

Modern man's treatment of wildlife may leave a lot to be desired, but

Bluebell

Tawny owl

things are better than they were fifty years ago. In the days of intensely keepered estates, any bird with a hooked bill was shot, poisoned or cruelly trapped. The barbaric pole trap is now thank goodness outlawed, but still used by the occasional ignoramus. Young (sometimes not so young) people still occasionally remove birds of prey from their nests in order to bring them up as pets. The diet they are given is invariably inadequate — it is difficult to feed a captive bird in any case — and death comes miserably and slowly. It was not realised until fairly recently when man became capable of disrupting wildlife on a grand scale just how delicately nature is balanced. A reduction in predators means increased populations of small birds and mammals, with a subsequent reduction in insect food available. The net result could be large populations of hungry creatures much more susceptible to epidemic diseases, and an insect population too small to pollinate the flowers. You disrupt food chains at your peril!

In a typical oak or oak—ash wood the dominant plant in the shrub layer is hazel. Guelder rose, wayfaring tree, holly and blackthorn may all occur with some frequency, but the nut-tree holds sway. Its prominence in vegetational history is shown by the frequency of its pollen in the 'boreal period' deposits, indicating that it dominated most of Europe in this period, and its place in human history by the voluminous folklore surrounding it. *Corylus avellana* never assumes

Pole trap (*RSPB*)

the dominating stature of a tree, but it was probably better known to our sylvan-orientated ancestors than most larger species because of its nuts. It was thought in times gone by to have the ability to detect or divine metals, and indeed is still used by some to divine water. John Evelyn wrote somewhat sceptically of such beliefs current in his time:

> ...and divinatory rods for the detecting and finding out of minerals; at least, if that tradition be no imposture. By whatsoever occult virtue the forked stick, so cut and skilfully held, becomes impregnated with those invisible streams and exhalations, as by its spontaneous bending from a horizontal posture to discover not only mines and subterraneous treasure, and springs of water, but criminals guilty of murder etc., made out so solemnly by the attestation of magistrates, and divers other learned and credible persons, who have critically examined matters of fact, is certainly next to a miracle, and requires a strong faith.

Hazel nuts face assault from all sides. Grey squirrels, mice and nuthatches bash, gnaw and nibble through the shells, whilst the tiny weevil *Circulio nucum* makes a much more subtle but equally effective approach. Guided by some stimulus not yet fully understood the female weevil seeks out the developing nut while it is still soft. She easily drills a neat hole in the shell (close examination of hazel nuts will reveal them) and lays a single egg, which remains dormant until the kernel within enlarges. Once the food supply is sufficient a white grub emerges from the egg and consumes the kernel. When ready to complete its development the grub is able to bore its way out of the hard shell, after which it falls to the ground and pupates in the soil. The following summer the pupa case splits to allow the adult weevil to emerge, seek a mate, copulate and thus perpetuate the species. *Circulio* has no vernacular name, but perhaps we may be allowed to invent one, the hazel-nut weevil.

Differences between the two British species of oak

	COMMON OR PEDUNCULATE (*Quercus robur*)	DURMAST OR SESSILE (*Quercus petraea*)
DISTRIBUTION	South-east, Midlands; deep loamy soils preferred	North and West; sandy soils in South
ACORNS	Carried on a stalk; longitudinal green stripes on acorn	No stalk and no stripes
LEAVES	Have a short stalk, less than 10mm or absent, usually hairless	Stem prominent and up to 25mm long; hairy, at least on underside
BUDS	Small, brown, blunt	Larger, sharper, but also brown

Oak wood is now the natural woodland over a large proportion of Britain. Following an initial pioneering period by birch and pine, oak assumed almost complete dominance. At altitudes above 400 metres and in areas of shallow, mineral-deficient soils, however, oak does not thrive and here birch and pine can retain their dominance. There are two species of oak indigenous to Britain, the common or pedunculate oak (*Quercus robur*) and the durmast or sessile oak (*Quercus petraea*). Their differences are summarised in the table, but where they grow together hybridisation is so frequent that they are often difficult to distinguish. Because of the oak's great value as a timber tree, many of our oak woods are only semi-natural, resulting from panic-stricken replanting following wholesale felling. Present-day oak woods are of the 'coppice-with-standard' variety, where the oaks are well spaced to allow straight growth in full sunlight. In this system, the shrub layer of hazel is cut back to stools at approximately ten-year intervals. This allows light to reach the field layer, which consequently can be very rich. Following the replacement of wood by ferrous metals for shipbuilding, when many of these woodlands were totally neglected, some were used for indiscriminate shooting by well-to-do, nothing-to-do 'sportsmen' who shot anything and everything, even being

The two species of oak in Britain: sessile (above) and pedunculate (below)

prepared on occasions 'to smoke the blighters out'. The importance of these woods as wildlife refuges is now realised. They are home to many birds, including green and great spotted woodpeckers, tree-creepers, nuthatches, willow warblers, whitethroats, chiff-chaffs, woodcocks, wrens, redstarts, flycatchers, jays, magpies and a host of others, not least the titmice. Oak woods are fruitful hunting grounds for those who tread quietly and carry binoculars in preference to guns.

Small mammals, too, find a variety of food to sustain them for the whole year, feeding not only on the ground-dwelling insects but also on those which drop from the canopy which in oak supports a thriving community of its own. Shrews, for example, relish the winter-moth pupae which develop in the soil from caterpillars that gorged themselves on oak leaves in the summer. In the course of one year watching a northern oak—ash wood, I identified the pygmy shrew, common shrew, long-tailed field mouse, bank vole and both hedgehog and mole. The latter two species were originally inhabitants of deciduous woodlands but the hedgehog found man's hedges much to its liking and adapted quickly to tree clearance, whilst the mole adapted even more quickly, finding burrowing decidedly less strenuous under a field than beneath the woodland floor criss-crossed with twisted roots of trees. I found our native red squirrel in some numbers, but, at least in the north, no sign yet of the larger grey squirrel — introduced from North America during the second half of the nineteenth century, and now so common in many parts of the country. Predators of these small mammals include stoat, weasel, badger and red fox. Badgers are surprisingly partial to hedgehogs and may account for the absence of them in southern oak woods. I found no sign of polecat or pine marten, although the former may still be found in Wales and the latter in the Lake District and in Scotland, increasingly so with the proliferation of young conifer plantations. Finally I also recorded rabbit, hare, roe deer and red deer in my woodland. The rabbit is not native to this country, but the other three were inhabitants of the ancient forests and learned to adapt to loss of habitat by a combination of wit and fleetness of foot. Survival, however, proved to be beyond the powers of the more hunted species—wild boar, brown bear, beaver and that persecuted wolf.

The oak of course had its part in folklore. The Greek name for a tree was *drys*, the Celtic being *derw*, but this referred specifically to the oak. The druids, the priests of the Celts, obviously derived their names from the oaks beneath whose branches they preached. Once each year, in worship to the gods, all the fires belonging to the population at large were extinguished and relighted from the sacred, and allegedly perpetual, fire of the druids. This is the origin of the Yule log which became integrated into our Christmas celebrations. Yule

Red squirrel

logs were generally of oak, but ash was sometimes used, and this reflects the preponderance of mixed oak—ash woods in northern parts. The druid ceremonies under oaks were doubtless intended to mystify the onlookers, but those priests of the wildwoods had a full and working knowledge of the wildlife contained within their extensive temple. No doubt, though, they were prepared to sacrifice some truth in order to add to the mystique of their ceremonies: the apparent gathering of mistletoe from oak branches is a case in point, since this semi-parasitic plant is seldom found on oak, preferring to suck the juices of lesser species such as crab apple and poplar. Great ritual accompanied the gathering of this sacred plant. Having no doubt hidden a supply earlier in the day, they went into the oak groves which had to be bathed in moonlight. The mistletoe had to be cut with a golden knife and never be allowed to fall to the ground. The plant seems to have had two uses; the main one was to ward off witchcraft and sprigs were often worn round the neck for protection. The other was as some sort of aid to fertility, and this is obviously the origin of 'kissing under the mistletoe'. Mistletoe was also an important part of the garland of Jack-in-the-Green or the Green Man, the traditional representation of spring; the dance of the may was a fertility rite and the maypole a phallic symbol.

As the druids were pushed further westward and northward the Saxons were bequeathed a Celtic symbolism which survives to this day, as do some important items of Celtic oaken furniture. Two pieces have particular interest: the so-called King Arthur's round table and the cradle of the future King Edward II. He was born in Caernarvon Castle and his cradle was fashioned of oak in the hope of pleasing the Welsh, who retained more than a touch of superstition regarding the powers of oak, left over from their Celtic ancestors.

Beech Woods

I did think of being controversial and omitting beech from my list of British woodlands, because it has a much more restricted distribution than the oak. The pollen record indicates that beech once had a firmer grip on these islands, except Ireland which it never seems to have reached by natural means. It will grow in the north, but mostly likes the warmer chalkland soils in the more south-easterly areas. In the colder weather conditions of the north-west, it may fail to set sufficient seed to be able to become a dominant tree.

The dense foliage of simple, delicate green but overlapping leaves imparts a very heavy shade, and the tall, smooth, grey, column-like trunks give a beech wood the tranquil air of a mellowed cathedral. The

Beech trees—Barden near Burnley

wide naves and side chapels are not cluttered with shrub or field layers, since the shade prevents it; furthermore, beech leaves decay very slowly and thus deny light even to the hardy bryophytes, although a couple of species, *Polytrichum formosum* and *Leucobryum glaucum*, seem to have overcome these problems. Under these conditions several fungi also thrive. Few have vernacular names, though the death cap (*Amanita phalloides*) is well enough known, at least by reputation, considering that it is our most deadly fungus. *Armillaria mucida* (beech fungus), *Amanita vaginata, Russula lepida, Russula fellea* and *Hericium coralloides* are a few others from a long list.

Because of the poorly developed lower layers there is little attraction for birds in a pure beech wood: both nest sites and suitable food are relatively scarce. In winter, great tit, blue tit, chaffinch and its winter-visiting cousin the brambling, feed on beech mast, but even this is not a reliable source of support. In 'mast years' there may be a veritable glut of beech nuts, but for several seasons together the crop may totally fail. It is possible that the beech has evolved the tendency to produce rich crops and poor crops in alternate years to outwit the birds, preventing large populations surviving from one winter to the next and demolishing the trees' seed output.

Pine Woods

The Scots pine (*Pinus sylvestris*) is Britain's only indigenous conifer capable of forming a pure woodland in its own right, but it often forms a mixed wood with birch. 'Our' species is one of the commonest of the European pines and the pollen record shows that it was one of the dominant trees in more than one post-glacial period. In southern Britain *Pinus sylvestris* was superseded by the oak, but in Scotland it was able to survive for centuries. With the Industrial Revolution, the insatiable demands for timber from south of the border resulted in ruthless exploitation with no thought for conservation of stocks. Regeneration of the forests was prevented by yet another insatiable demand, this time for wool: even where forest was not cleared to make way for sheep, the succulent pine seedlings were browsed, leaving only bracken and heather to dominate the area.

By 1975 the truly native Scottish pine woods numbered only about thirty-five, varying from small clumps of trees to small forests of 200–300 hectares (one hectare is equal to about 2½ acres). Some of these trees were estimated to be over 300 years old. Recognising the value of these relict areas, which have persisted with little disturbance

Beech

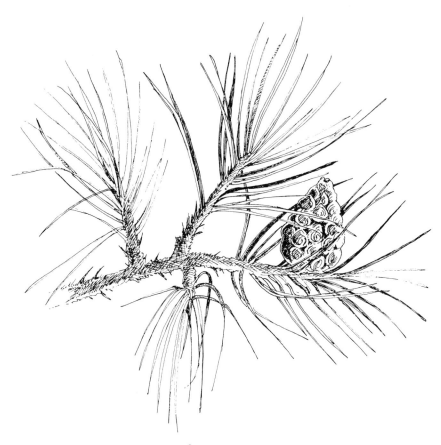

Scots pine

since the close of the last Ice Age, scientists organised a symposium at Aviemore in 1975, and a report entitled *Native Pinewoods of Scotland* was published by the Institute of Terrestrial Ecology in 1977. Britain's woodlands have surely reached and passed their lowest ebb: conservation is an 'in' word and government now listens more attentively to ecological argument. These pine woods are of great interest to the ecologist, not least because so many rare beetles are unique to this environment. Because of the perpetual shade in some woods the layering I have been describing for other woodlands does not exist, and fungi again hold a dominant position. *Hypholoma fasciculare* (sulphur tuft), *Armillaria mellea* (honey fungus) and *Collybria peronata* (wood woolly-foot) grow saprophytically upon fallen pine needles and therefore do no harm and even do good by speeding up decomposition. The fly agaric also grows in pine woods, forming mycorrhizal relationships, as with birch. Other fungi feed parasitically upon pines and can do substantial damage. *Polyporus*

Juniper

(*Phaeolus*) *schweinitzii* is one such species — a large reddish-brown toadstool found growing near the base of the trunk and causing fatal 'heart-rot'.

Many of the Scottish pine woods however are quite open and allow some shrubs to flourish, prominent among them the juniper whose berries are used to flavour gin, and whose timber was burned to produce extra-powerful gunpowder — savin powder. The only other common member of the shrub layer is the red-berried rowan or mountain ash. Flowers include the pink-flowered lesser wintergreen, and the double pink flowers of the twinflower, confined to the highland woods of north-eastern Scotland. The list is not long, but includes tormentil, heath bedstraw, wavy hair grass and two interesting orchids, the quite common creeping lady's tresses and the much rarer coral-root orchid, *Corallorhiza trifida*, a saprophytic feeder having few green leaves. A fungus is associated with the coral-like roots, and whilst this is not a true mycorrhizal relationship it is without doubt symbiotic.

Crested tit

To a naturalist, a reference to a pine wood immediately brings two animals to mind, the crested tit and the red squirrel. Newton and Moss, however, discovered at least seventy bird species breeding in Scottish pine woods. In *Native Pinewoods of Scotland* they report:

24 species depend on openings for feeding or nesting, and 13 others on water, either streams or lochs. Of the four corvids, crows are widespread while magpies and jays are local, but all three would be commoner if they were persecuted less by gamekeepers. Among the six seed eaters the chaffinch is common everywhere, the greenfinch is local near farmland while the bullfinch breeds mainly in areas of Juniper. The number of crossbills and siskins fluctuates greatly from year to year, according to the size of the local pine crop, and the number of redpolls according to the birch crop (Newton 1972). The crossbills of northern Scotland form a distinct race (*Loxia curvirostra scotica*) feeding almost entirely from pine cones; they are larger, with heavier bills than the nominate *Loxia curvirostra curvirostra* which feed largely on seeds from the softer spruce cones... of 26 insectivorous song birds the commonest are the wren,

willow warbler (a summer visitor), goldcrest and coal tit. In general the coal tit outnumbers the crested by 3 or 4 to 1 (Nethersole-Thompson and Watson 1974) and whilst the former can nest among stones and logs on the ground, the latter requires soft rotten tree stumps and is thus largely absent from newer plantations.

Some lessons here are clear. Once the new plantations mature, careful management would allow a greater variety of bird life — for example by leaving the odd tree stump as habitat for the crested tit. Nowadays, both the Forestry Commission and private planters, on the whole, realise the value of a healthy stock of wild creatures.

My concluding remarks regarding Britain's woodlands must be optimistic. The vast areas in Scotland and the North once clothed in trees were thoughtlessly cleared. The ground without trees became waterlogged and acidic. However, the roots of conifers can dry out these areas once more and make the ground able to support deciduous woodlands in time. The young plantations allow hen harriers, short-eared owls and even redwings to breed, and favour the spread of former inhabitants like the pine marten and wild cat. Mature stands are once more providing nesting habitat for the osprey, extinct in this country from the late nineteenth century till the 1950s. Added to this, a reduction in the senseless killing of raptors has made the bleak outlook for Britain's wildlife rather brighter.

On a global scale, things do not look so good. Our woodland stocks are the lowest in Europe, forcing us to make substantial imports of timber from abroad, thus reducing timber stocks elsewhere. This fact should not be left out of sight, out of mind, for the whole world's tree resources must be watched. Plants produce oxygen, as a result of photosynthesis, and the more trees we have the richer is the world's oxygen balance. An energy crisis, a financial crisis, indeed any sort of crisis, is preferable to an oxygen crisis. Trees are not just decorative and nice for the birds: they mean life itself to mankind and all the rest of the animal kingdom.

3
The Hedge

The familiar patchwork quilt of the British landscape today is largely a product of the eighteenth-century enclosures, the 'seams' are the hedgerows put in to divide the commons into fields. We tend to associate hedges with shrubby growth like hawthorn and blackthorn but a great deal of tree planting also typified the enclosure movement — elm, especially over much of southern and eastern England, beech on Exmoor; at least before the advent of Dutch elm disease, almost half the hardwood timber in England was growing in hedgerows. In the course of time other species colonised hedges, creating a haven for wildlife, establishing a healthy food chain. On the sunlit hedgebanks many herbaceous plants found ideal conditions, attracting in turn a diverse insect community, including some of our most cherished butterflies. The varied fare of insects, berries and seeds supports birds and small mammals. The unrivalled wealth invested in hedgerows as wildlife refuges has been seriously eroded by modern farming practices which call for wide open spaces, although this may prove, in the long run, to be a false economy to agriculture. If anything more need convince us of the importance of conserving the hedge, we need only remind ourselves that an estimate in the early 1960s put the coverage of hedges in Britain — nearly half a million acres — at twice that of the country's officially declared nature reserves.

One of my earliest memories concerns my Cornish great-grandmother who had removed to Cumbria (then the Furness district of Lancashire) with her husband who was a miner. Apart from her quaint speech I remember the amusement when she referred to local stone walls as hedges. In fact the dictionary definition of a hedge says 'a fence of bushes or small trees'. This is probably what most of us would accept, but the further definition of a hedge is 'a barrier of any kind'. The old Cornish lady was right. Any structure used to fence in crops or cattle, and also to fence out destructive wildlife, is a true hedge. On the island of St Kilda there are no trees, but 'hedges' of stone were constructed to confine the Soay sheep. In the *Anglo-Saxon*

Typical hedge system, at Chipping near Preston

Chronicle of AD 547 there is a record of Ida of Northumbria constructing a hedge around his settlement at Bamburgh in Northumberland. Surviving contemporary records are naturally sparse, but King Ine of Wessex is stated to have constructed a fence to protect crops from cattle. This document is dated AD 690.

How these ancient hedges were constructed and of what material is not known. The tendency however seems to have been to construct a 'dead hedge' in preference to a modern 'quick hedge', for which trees or bushes are deliberately planted around a desired area of land and allowed to grow naturally before being trimmed. Many other live hedges probably represent surviving strips of natural woodland which were left as windbreaks and boundaries between fields. The dead hedge made of cut timber is now a thing of the past, although at Whitby in North Yorkshire the techniques of its construction have been handed down in a tradition which began in 1315. This resulted from a fable

concerning three noblemen, who went out on a wild-boar hunt near the town. They inflicted severe wounds on the animal, which after a long and exhausting chase through the tangled undergrowth sought sanctuary in a hermitage occupied by a monk from Whitby. The worthy cleric seems to have been a fourteenth-century conservationist and attempted to intercede on behalf of the wounded animal; he was thrashed by the noblemen for his interference. The incident was reported to the abbot, who flew into a rage and was about to hand out heavy punishment, when the fatally injured monk demonstrated his Christian beliefs by, metaphorically at least, turning the other cheek. He asked for mercy on behalf of his assailants. The abbot moderated the punishment and commanded them to 'go to the woods of Strayhead (on Ascension Eve) in Eskdaleside, cut stakes and rods, then carry them to Whitby and build a dead hedge on the foreshore of sufficient strength to stand three tides'. All the lands of the offenders would be forfeit should they, or their descendants, fail to carry out this penance to the full every year.

But a dead hedge constructed to delineate a field system or protect a dwelling would soon rot away, and would be of no use to wildlife. Some of the advantages of the quick hedge, and the essential techniques for its construction, were realised, at least on the continent, before the birth of Christ: to quote from Caesar's *Gallic War*:

> The Nervii [a tribe living on the borders of France and Belgium], in order that they might more easily obstruct their neighbours' cavalry who came down on them for plunder, half cut young trees, bent them over and interwove branches among them, and with brambles and young thorns growing up, these hedges present a barrier like a wall which is not only impossible to penetrate, but also impossible to see through.

This type of hedge provides ideal cover for the herbivorous animal, the perfect wildlife sanctuary, and the fact that there is often open grassland on either side means that a rich food supply is close at hand and can be consumed in relative safety.

As we have seen in previous chapters, woodland and unenclosed common land was still the rule during the middle ages and hedges a definite exception. The Lord of the Manor had however fenced off his own lands since the time of the Conqueror. Within these boundary limits his underlings strove to produce food using the 'open-field system'. (This can still be seen in operation at Laxton in Nottinghamshire.) The fields were divided into strips, and each worker was allotted several, in different parts of the area so that each had a share of the most fertile land.

In 1348 the Black Death — brought back, so it is said, by returning

Building a stone hedge on the lakeland fells

Crusaders — killed large numbers of people, and it is thought that a shortage of manpower affected the countryside. One solution for landowners bereft of workers was to have less acreage under plough — to enclose fields by hedges and graze sheep therein. The mass of hedges, however, were not planted until after the eighteenth-century Enclosure Acts; to some extent they compensated for the loss of woodlands, where wildlife was concerned. As we have seen woodland edges are especially rich habitats and broad hedges re-create many of the same conditions. Even animals of retiring character were able to adjust more easily to the loss of deciduous woodland if hedges were there for refuge.

When a forest was devastated for its timber, it was seldom consumed from one end to the other. The best timber would be selected and felled, leaving many trees standing. The result would be a series of small woods separated by quite wide open spaces. Animals and birds could survive quite well in the cover of small woods, but would have been much more vulnerable when, in their search for food or nest sites, they had to cross the open spaces. The development of quick hedges meant that animals could leave a small wood while still keeping hidden from predators. The hedgerow is not only a wildlife sanctuary in its own right, but also serves as a sort of motorway linking woodland 'townships'. As an example, the tiny wren makes much use of this arboreal highway.

The majority of the Enclosure Acts — there were over 5,000 to cover local situations — date from the Hanoverian monarchs, the first three Georges, but the original one dates from 1603 and the last, at Skipworth in Yorkshire, became law exactly 300 years later. Most of our hedges are therefore Georgian in origin but there are some of great antiquity; some of these marked parish boundaries. Pollard, Hooper and Moore have devised a system of dating hedges, which although not precise, has proved to be a good indication. As a hedgerow ages, more and more species gradually become established in it, so the main part of the exercise is to find out how many shrub species there are. A section of the hedge to be investigated, which looks fairly typical and not too close to the edge, is selected. A distance of about 25 metres (30 yards) is marked out. The hedge is then examined from one side only and the number of different species of shrubs and trees of mature age are counted. Seedlings are ignored. The age of the hedge is then estimated by substitution in the equation:

$$\text{Age of hedge} = (99 \times \text{number of species}) - 16 \text{ years}$$

Thus if hawthorn, maple, ash and hazel were found, we would have a hedge of $99 \times 4 - 16$ or 380 years. No one, least of all the originators of

Building a dead hedge at Chipping

the method, claims absolute reliability, but checks made by reference to old maps bear out its usefulness.

Dudley Stamp in his book *Man and the Land*, published in 1953, came up with a figure for the total length of our hedges that is now considered to be an over-estimate, but even allowing for a reduction in his 1,500,000 miles, the area concerned must be a considerable wildlife reservoir. In recent years the proliferation of mechanised farm equipment and the sowing of cereal monocultures have led to considerable clearance of hedges in intensive farming areas as farmers have wished to enlarge the working area for their combine-harvesters; estimates have been made that around 5,000 miles per annum are being lost. The dimensions of many fields, though, were originally determined by the work capacity of a one-man horse-ploughing team and obviously cannot always be right for today's conditions. With the growing shortage of fossil fuels it has been suggested there might possibly be some return to the horse and plough, reducing the destruction of hedges, and perhaps even encouraging more; but this seems mere townsman's nostalgia.

Hedges for Today

Those who earn a living from the land are entitled to ask 'What is the use of a hedge?' Apart from its importance to wildlife, it has another vital function today. A farmer's most valuable asset is his soil; one of the most destructive factors affecting soil is a combination of dry weather and high wind. If soil is blown about unchecked, it will leave a desert area, too thinly covered to support crops. Some sort of windbreak is essential to long-term soil fertility. Hedgerows also provide shelter for many animals that can benefit the farmer. Predatory spiders, for example, help to keep down destructive insects like aphids which in most years are one of the main factors reducing the yield of cereal crops. Our farming system, despite views often expressed to the contrary, is as efficient as any in Europe, and one of the main reasons for this is our hedgerow system.

No discussion of British hedgerows would be complete without reflecting the complaint of many of the older generation of naturalists, who often say that our hedgerows are not as attractive as they used to be. There is evidence that this is not just another case of the memories of childhood being bathed in golden nostalgia. In many areas since the 1950s the policy of spraying hedgerows to keep down 'untidy' undergrowth has destroyed many of our more beautiful hedgerow flowers. Some of the British hedgerows are now little more than a boring monoculture of hardier plants such as the coarsely conspicuous

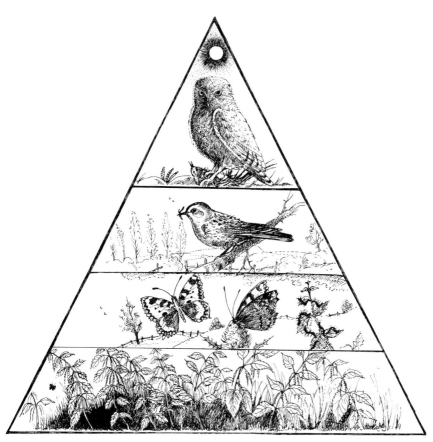

Food pyramid for hedgerows with (top to bottom) little owl, dunnock, small tortoiseshell butterfly and plants

hogweed. Many problems facing conservationists today have either no solution at all, or present complex difficulties; but this particular problem can be solved easily enough. Do we want clinically neat hedgerows, with only empty cigarette packets and cans at their edges, or do we save money on poisonous sprays and allow the local plants to creep back and redecorate with a riot of colour? A look at a food pyramid will show the far-reaching damage caused by indiscriminate spraying.

The hedgerow is full of wildlife, and as always every species depends to some degree on others. The herbicides sprayed upon the vegetation break the food chain in its very early stages, reducing the food available for insects. In turn, there are fewer insect larvae on which the small birds such as robins, wrens, chaffinches and dunnocks can feed their young. Thus the adults abandon their nesting attempts, or young birds starve to death in the nest, and the population of small birds declines. The reduction in insect food will also adversely affect the population of small mammals — voles, mice and shrews. The top carnivores now begin to feel the pangs of hunger. Barn owls, sparrowhawks, kestrels, also foxes, weasels and stoats, must all be harder pressed. If any of these should seek better pickings around farms, the farming community, naturally, declares war on 'vermin', and thus more of our beleaguered wildlife is attacked for trying to stay alive. The more dangerous fungicides, herbicides and insecticides used by farmers are rarely selective, and kill even species positively beneficial to mankind, as well as indirectly affecting all by damaging the food chain.

Though toxic chemicals, such as those in mercury-based fungicidal seed-dressings, are applied in concentrations too weak to kill most birds directly, they are passed on to birds through the insects and seeds they eat, and gradually accumulate in their tissues. Again, though few birds die directly from this absorption, there are sinister side-effects. A great deal of evidence supports the claim that DDT and other so-called 'chlorinated hydrocarbons' disrupt the bird's breeding cycle so that it lays thin-shelled eggs which collapse on incubation, or fails to incubate them properly so that they become chilled and fail to hatch. This has been a major source of breeding failure in sparrowhawks, peregrine falcons and other raptors, and also in fish-eating birds in freshwater habitats. Such birds are especially vulnerable by virtue of being at the top of the food pyramid. The lower echelons absorb much smaller quantities; it is as these small quantities are passed on to, and concentrated in, their predators, as we ascend the food chain, that the poison loads increase, up to the top carnivores. Long-lived birds, they have plenty of time to pick up heavy toxic loads.

Another interesting suggestion has recently been made. It is known that large numbers of birds perish during cold winters, but it does seem that more have died in recent severe spells than did so in similar conditions a hundred years ago. Even allowing for the greater density of bird watchers and the consequent discovery of more bodies, it still seems that birds do not cope as well with a cold winter as they did in years gone by. Poisons can accumulate in a bird's body fat as well as in other tissues, such as the liver and brain; when food is plentiful this reserve fat is not drawn upon, but when cold weather strikes and this store has to be mobilised, it is possible that the poisons are released into the bloodstream. This might provide the final coup-de-grâce to a bird already weakened by hunger.

Once again the 1980s allow some optimism. Many local authorities have reduced the amount of roadside spraying they do — if only because they can no longer afford it. Then, the extremely harmful chemicals of the 1950s and 60s, notably DDT, dieldrin and aldrin, are banned and many of the birds they undermined, notably sparrowhawks and peregrines, are doing much better. The successors to these toxins are safer and the use of biological control in place of chemical methods is a little better understood. This involves a detailed study of a pest and all aspects of its natural history including its predators, so that natural food chains can be manipulated to man's advantage. In the event of an abnormally high population of pests the appropriate predator can be introduced to help with the problem. Obviously this can sometimes be impossible and often expensive, but the more we learn about it the more chance it has of success. Although biological control has scored some spectacular successes in other parts of the world (eg the elimination of the troublesome prickly-pear cactus in Australia by a caterpillar introduced from America), it has so far only limited application in Britain. Anyone who needs a more familiar example than prickly pear need only recall the impact of the ladybird outbreak in the 1976 drought on the equally prolific aphids which are its main prey. It is a familiar story that after the construction of the Crystal Palace in 1851, house sparrows invaded the building and all too frequently 'whitewashed' important visitors. Queen Victoria called in the Duke of Wellington to advise; 'Try sparrowhawks, ma'am,' he said. Biological control is not a new idea!

The Natural History of the Hedge

Since so many hedges originated as woodland remnants — and are often virtually woodlands in strip form — all trees occurring in our woods are also found in hedges. The most widespread hedgerow tree is the hawthorn. The land-enclosure movement in the eighteenth century turned enthusiastically to hawthorn for containing livestock. Thousands of miles were planted, and once established the shrub lasts a long time. The dense robust hedges were painful to breach and relatively unpalatable, not only to livestock but also to rabbits, which are so destructive to shrubs with poorer defences. Another species to evolve a good strategy against browsing and gnawing creatures is the ubiquitous elder, whose bark is a violent purgative to man, and doubtless to rabbits as well, judging by the elders that can flourish in the midst of their warrens. The elm is, or was, one of the most typical trees of southern hedges; other common species include the blackthorn (or sloe), field maple, spindle, hazel, holly, hornbeam, dog rose and crab apple. Botanical hedgerows are much more typical of southern England; many other parts of the British Isles have drystone-wall 'hedges'.

The hawthorn (*Crataegus monogyna*) is a small shrub or tree — it

82

seldom grows taller than 30 feet (10 metres). The sweet-smelling white flowers, borne at the ends of short leafy shoots, are the 'may' flowers, alleged to bring ill luck if brought into the house. The leaves appear on the prickly branches before the flowers, in contrast to those of the blackthorn (*Prunus spinosa*). Each flower has many stamens but only a single style, with the stigma having a pronounced 'knob'. Each of the haws, the red fruits that hang in such rich bunches in autumn, contains a single 'stone' or seed surrounded by a fleshy coat, good food for hungry birds, especially in winter. The indigestible seed passes out in their droppings, thus effectively dispersing the species; furthermore the seeds of eaten haws are not only carried afar, but actually start to germinate sooner (up to a year earlier) than uneaten ones, a consequence of being exposed to the digestive process. It is easy to appreciate why trees like the hawthorn have evolved brightly coloured berries to attract birds.

The Midland hawthorn (*Crataegus oxyacanthoides*) is a much more uncommon species, usually confined to clay soils in the east of England and even then preferring woodland habitats. The leaves are less deeply cut and the blossom much less prolific. A close look at the structure of the flower reveals the presence of two or three styles, not one as in the commoner species, so each haw contains two, or even three, seeds.

The common hawthorn still enjoys a prominent place in tree folklore. It was, and to a certain extent still is, associated with the village festivities of 1 May; indeed may-bush is the old name for the species. A bunch of may blossom was an essential decoration both for the maypole and for the May Queen's crown, while the Lord of the May, her husband, was dressed in oak. The may-blossom was always in bloom in time for this ancient ceremony until the year 1752, when the New Style calendar was introduced! May 13 is now the first realistic date on which more than odd sprays of hawthorn blossom can be expected. Both Greeks and Romans seem to have regarded the hawthorn as a symbol of hope, and in the wedding processions a torch of hawthorn preceded the bride. It has been traditionally assumed that the soldiers made Christ's crown of thorns from hawthorn; in France the belief was so well instilled in country people's minds that until fairly recently some believed that groaning noises issued from the hawthorn on Good Friday.

Perhaps the most extravagant claim for the mystic merits of the species centres on the Glastonbury thorn — though similar connections have been made between hawthorns and other religious traditions. The usual version of the legend is that when Joseph of

Hawthorn

Arimathaea came to convert the inhabitants of Britain, accompanied by the requisite number of apostles (twelve), he landed at Avalon (Glastonbury). Fatigued by the sea journey the venerable missionary stuck his old hawthorn staff in the ground and drifted off to sleep. When he awoke (presumably the next morning), he found that his staff had both rooted and blossomed. Joseph took what he thought was a hint from the Almighty and set up his headquarters at Glastonbury, where the hawthorn bush — or its descendant — continues to bloom annually at the time of landing, which was, incidentally, December.

Another historical anecdote concerns the hawthorn's association with the house of Tudor. After the Battle of Bosworth in 1485, the body of Richard III was stripped almost naked and his own crown dragged from his head and hurled into a hawthorn bush. The father-in-law of Henry Tudor, Lord Stanley, retrieved it and placed it on the head of Henry VII and the house of Tudor was born. The Tudors hereafter used as their emblem a crown nestling in a hawthorn tree full of berries. A proverb, 'Cleave to the crown though it hangs in a bush', obviously dates to this period.

In Henry VIII's time hordes of folk would enthusiastically celebrate May Day by going out the day before into the villages surrounding London, to Highgate and Hampstead, Greenwich and Fulham, Southwark, Shooters Hill and scores of other hamlets, spending the night (or at least part of it!) cutting down branches from the may tree, selecting a tall tree to trim for the maypole and gathering flowers to decorate it. The pole was dragged through the streets by a spruced-up team of muscled oxen accompanied , by prancing merrymakers. Doubtless much ale would be drunk, many pockets would be picked, a few maidenheads sacrificed, as the warm days of summer were thus ushered in.

The first syllable of 'hawthorn' is a corruption of *hage* or *hoeg*, and thus it was even named hedge-thorn. The Greeks' three names for it were Crataegus, oxyacantha and pyracantha; the Roman word for it was spina, which leads to the question of the difference between a thorn and a prickle. A rose prickle, for example, can be prised away from the stem to leave a small scar, showing that there is no intimate connection with the interior tissues of the plant. Thorns, however, are more like mini-branches. They increase in size each year, they carry leaves and are protected with their own bark and other essential tissues. Prickles never grow into branches in their own right. Our own British names include the already-mentioned may-bush, quickthorn and quickset (referring to its use as a living hedge, as opposed to the earlier traditional dead hedge). Whitethorn is sometimes a misleading name since as the blossoms fade they become distinctly pink, although the early fresh-spring-flush is white as a snowdrift.

The hawthorn and the Battle of Bosworth

Wren searching for Chinese character moth

Hawthorn flower is certainly fragrant — I once asked half a dozen friends what the smell reminded them of. Their answers were interesting if not very helpful: fish (three times), rotten fish (once) and 'like dew on roses' (twice)! I think this says more about the accuracy of the human sense of smell than it does about the perfume of hawthorn. Bio-chemists have analysed the chemical responsible as being trimethylamine.

Though the spiny twigs confound would-be gnawers and browsers, hawthorn has palatable leaves and fruit, which make it popular with many forms of wildlife, both vertebrate and invertebrate. It has been present in Britain from the very earliest times, and so wild creatures have had ample time to learn to use it to the full. Almost 100 species of

Wren

moth will eat the leaves, one of the most bizarre being the Chinese-character moth (*Cilix glaucata*), which has evolved to resemble unpalatable bird-droppings. In winter, resident blackbirds and thrushes, along with immigrant waxwings, redwings and fieldfares, depend upon the hawthorn berries to keep body and soul together, as do bank voles and wood mice which climb the branches to reach them. In summer, thick thorn hedges provide nesting sites for many small birds, as well as bigger ones like the jay, magpie and woodpigeon. Spiny thickets make excellent roosting sites, safe from predators, for legions of birds, sometimes hundreds of thousands of starlings.

The elm (*Ulmus procera*) never forms a woodland in its own right, but with the Enclosure Acts landowners often insisted that tenant farmers should plant it at intervals along hawthorn hedges: the object was both to yield timber and to enhance the look of the landscape. The tree was easily propagated from cuttings, spread itself conveniently along the row by sucker roots and grew rapidly to majestic proportions, furnishing a versatile timber for all sorts of domestic uses. Elm thus quickly established itself as a major hedgerow tree, towering above hawthorn and other bushes, making an indelible mark

(left to right) Elm fruit, leaves and flowers

on the English landscape — or so it was thought. With hindsight it is easy to see that a greater variety of hedge species would have been less vulnerable; in many parts of England today the elm is a fast-disappearing species due to the ravages of the infamous Dutch elm disease.

The disease has in fact been known for many years; Loudon, in 1838, mentioned that it was carried by a beetle which fed upon rotten wood. It seems first to have been noticed as early as 1818 but it was in Holland in 1919, the year that our Forestry Commission was set up, that it was finally named Dutch elm disease. Surveys were thought to be essential in Britain by the late 1920s, when it was already

Song thrush

widespread. Many of the trees were able to recover, and this naturally gave rise to complacency. However a new and more virulent strain reached Britain from North America about 1970, and in the seven years up to 1977 eleven million trees were destroyed, according to figures issued by the Forestry Commission, based on work done by Gibbs and Howell. In 1974 an Order was made prohibiting the movement of elm timber from diseased areas. Some curative treatments have been devised, but these are often prohibitively expensive and rarely effective, so the present policy is to let the disease take its course, and eventually as it has done in the past become less virulent. It has robbed many southern English hedges of much of their splendour.

The causative organism has been identified as a fungus, the name now accepted for it being *Ceratocystis ulmi*. It produces a substance which causes the cell walls of the elm to produce, as a defence against further fungal invasion, sticky swellings called tyloses; these block the vessels in the trunk of the tree which carry water to the leaves from the roots. Therefore the first signs of the disease will be a yellowing and then withering of the leaves due to water shortage and accounts for the fact that during hot summers like 1976 the effect is even more catastrophic.

The life history of the fungus was unravelled by painstaking work, mainly by Gibbs, and it is described in the Forestry Commission's Forest Record No 94 (published in 1974). Gibbs discovered two main types of reproduction. One is non-sexual and consists of tiny black stalks carrying swollen ends full of spores. The sexual process takes place again within the trunk of the tree: dark flask-shaped bodies produce 'eggs' and 'sperm' which eventually join together. Without the aid of a flying vector, however, the fungus would not spread rapidly enough to be a problem. Providing the transport is a bark beetle, *Scolytus scolytus* (sometimes, significantly, *Scolytus destructor*). This creature has become so infamous in recent years that it has been given the vernacular name of European elm-bark beetle. Male and female beetles bore their way through the bark to the sapwood. When the male has located a mate, presumably by chemical attraction rather than at random, he prepares a nuptial chamber. The female then lays about seventy eggs, from which hatch tiny legless white larvae. It seems that the fungus may be an important item in the diet of the grub. After five moults the larvae pupate, and in any warm spell from May to October the adults emerge from the pupae, bore their way outwards and fly off, probably carrying some fungus with them, in search of another elm tree. They settle on an elm and seem to give off a pheromone (chemical attractant) which brings along other beetles to continue the life cycle.

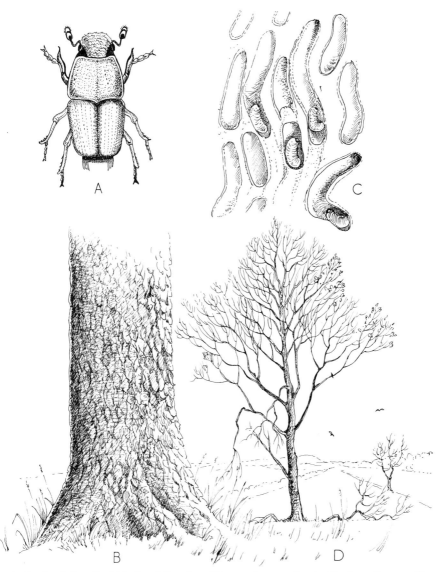

A elm bark beetle, B bole of the elm, C larvae burrowing in the tree tissues, D death of a roadside elm

Once a tree is dead, the hordes of beetle and other larvae in the rotting wood may temporarily benefit birds like woodpeckers and nuthatches, but the decaying canopy is no longer any use to the tits, warblers and other small birds that gleaned insects from its dense foliage. Rooks, kestrels, stock doves, little owls and tawny owls will all lose nest sites. As for the white-letter hairstreak butterfly, whose main food plant is the elm, the future must be bleak.

At one time it was thought that some types of elm were not susceptible to the disease but this is now discounted. We have eight fairly well marked species of elm, a larger number of local variants and a myriad of hybrids which makes the story complex. Following the end of the last Ice Age, elms were among the first arrivals. The hardiest, the wych elm (*Ulmus glabra*), is found throughout Britain, with a distinct preference for valley bottoms but also gracing the banks of Welsh streams and Scottish valleys. The further north you go, however, the smaller the tree becomes and the more urgently it seeks the shelter of the warmer valley floors. In the milder climate of the South the wych is free to spread its range and cover the landscape, often interbreeding with other species. But the English elm (*Ulmus procera*) is the one so typically part of the southern English landscape. As you move northwards it becomes much less common and probably any in Scotland were deliberately planted. The uses for this species were many and various, from cradles to coffins, furniture, water pipes and farm carts and waggons.

It is sometimes suggested that the English elm is not a true native but was introduced by the Romans — a theory based upon the fact that the species fails to produce viable seed; but modern scientific observations do not support this theory. The tree is a true endemic, because the roots produce suckers which grow upwards and develop into new trees, a sort of vegetative propagation not requiring the production of seeds. (This, incidentally, has hastened the demise of the elm from disease, since fungal infection can rapidly spread through the shared root system, as well as be transmitted by beetles.) It is also wrong to say that the species is completely sterile. The main reason for the failure of the seed to develop seems to be the very early flowering period, late frosts often killing the developing embryo. In warm springs — or should I say mild late winters — elm may well produce viable seeds and thus reproduce sexually as well as vegetatively.

Several other elm species may be found in certain limited areas, including the small-leaved elm (*Ulmus carpinifolia*), East Anglian elm (*Ulmus diversifolia*), Plot's elm (*Ulmus plotii*), Coritanian elm (*Ulmus coritani*), and Cornish elm (*Ulmus stricta*).

In the bottom of the hedgerow lurks a close relative of the elms and the unwary body will soon smart as a result of contact with it. The stinging nettle (*Urtica dioica*), which has been a very useful plant over the centuries, has actually proved very difficult to cultivate. This is because nettles demand nitrogen-rich soil. All members of the family have coarse fibres which can be converted into cloth — an analysis of captured German army uniforms in 1916 revealed that they consisted of 85 per cent nettle fibre. (Was it intended to attack the enemy with caterpillars?) It was also used as a green vegetable and was often grown commercially for this purpose. The stinging nettle, like the elm, has two methods of reproducing: the vegetative method, shoots springing up from underground rhizomes, and the sexual method, involving flowers of two types — male and female. (The *dioica* part of the scientific name derives from dioecious, meaning male and female).

To most people nettles are no longer a vital plant, merely a weed — weeds simply being plants growing where they are not wanted. Some years ago, helping to organise a nature centre and trail in a northern town, I wanted to encourage an extensive insect population, but was unable to convince the authorities that patches of nettles were beneficial; paraquat was squirted at them like monsoon rain and this was often followed by machines that hurled fire like the flames of hell. I quoted the work of Davies, who estimated that some twenty-seven species of insects in Britain are totally dependent upon nettle for their food. Obviously this also affects the birds, which either feed upon the insects themselves or on their larvae. Eventually the light dawned, people were stung as anticipated, and eleven species of insect new to the area were identified in four months.

Aphids, lacewings, ladybirds and moths are all of great interest to the entomologist, but for most people it is the conspicuous summery butterflies that typify hedgebanks strewn with nettles and other plants. The larvae of the small tortoiseshell and peacock eat nettles, the orange-tip and green-veined white seek garlic mustard, and the gatekeeper, wall and other browns love the long succulent grasses. Britain's butterflies are much rarer now and will only hold their own and perhaps begin to recover if our hedgerow plants are kept free from chemical interference.

One species which is still common is the showy and familiar small tortoiseshell butterfly (*Aglais urticae*). Its second scientific name indicates its close association with the nettle. The upper wings of the adult insect are basically bright reddish-brown, with variable patches of black, yellow and orange, the edges of both upper and lower wings bordered with blue crescents — the main distinguishing feature of a species easily identified by most of us. Two broods of eggs are produced per year, in May and in early July; they are laid on nettle leaves, on which the caterpillar feeds. It is covered with short dark hairs and when fully grown is basically yellowish with a black line down the dorsal surface. The tracheal system, through which caterpillars breathe, has an opening, a spiracle, in most body segments, and in this species these openings are black, ringed with yellow. The chrysalis is usually grey, but is often tinged pink. Like most butterflies the small tortoiseshell cannot remain active throughout the British winter and must therefore hibernate, which it does in

Small tortoiseshell butterfly

the adult stage, reappearing during the earliest days of spring.

It can be seen that the caterpillars of *Aglais urticae* form a link in the food chain between green plants and small birds.

One small bird which feeds on them is the dunnock, sometimes called the hedge sparrow. The dunnock (*Prunella modularis*) is a good example to represent the small bird community, its way of life, its ups and downs. Many birds will seek the shelter of a hedge, others will feed in it, yet others will nest within it, but none rely upon it so completely as the shy, often overlooked, dunnock. The adult bird is very secretive: its nest and eggs are much more familiar, as shown in the writings of Albin as long ago as 1759.

The bird is as well known as any of our small birds, being found in almost

Life history of the small tortoiseshell butterfly: A adult, B caterpillar, C pupa, D newly-emerged butterfly (the imago). All four stages have evolved excellent camouflage for living on nettles

Dunnock

every bush, that hardly a boy that searches the hedges but can give an
account of its nest and eggs etc; therefore it would seem unnecessary for me
to take any notice of it, but I think that the hedgesparrow is too much
neglected; no bird is more despised.

So it is today. Many know the delight of finding the beautiful blue
eggs, usually in groups of five, in the neat wool- or fur-lined nest. Few
can recognise the pleasant if rather thin-sounding song of spring.
Fewer can describe the bird's plumage and fewer still have watched
the parents feeding the caterpillars of the small tortoiseshell butterfly
to their gaping youngsters. Only the female incubates the eggs, which
hatch out in about thirteen days. The male then shares feeding duties
with his mate and the young can fly after eleven days, the short
breeding cycle allowing two or even three broods to be raised during a
reasonably clement summer. Quite a high proportion of nests are
parasitised by the cuckoo, but the association is an odd one, unlike
other cuckoo—host relationsips: the pale imposter does not resemble
the dunnock's own eggs, and yet it rarely gets ejected. The most
plausible explanation is that the dunnock is a relatively recent host of
the cuckoo, and neither party has had time to develop a very subtle
response to the other.

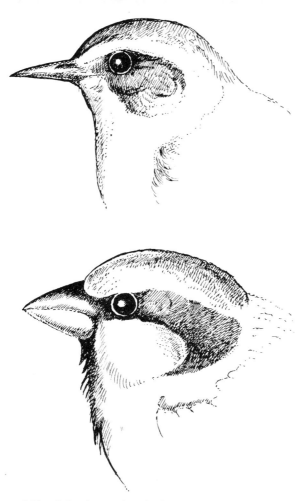

The different bills of the dunnock or hedge sparrow (above) and house sparrow
(below)

Though often known as the hedge sparrow, the dunnock bears no
relationship to the sparrows, as a glance at their relative bill structures
soon shows. The sparrow's powerful mandibles can cope with quite
large seeds, whilst that of the 'hedge sparrow' is much more suited for
coping with insects and small delicate seeds. The bird is an Accentor,
one of only two European species in the group, the other being the
Alpine Accentor (*Prunella collaris*). It has a large number of vernacular
names, including hedge grubber, shuffle wing, bush sparrow, creepie,
hedge betty, dyke sparrow, foolish sparrow, farmer's nightingale and
sugge. This latter name is thought to have been the origin of the place
names of Sugworth in Lancashire and Sugham in Surrey.

The dunnock is one of my favourite birds. Watching them gives me
an excuse to sit quietly in a hedgerow amongst the foxgloves and
greater bindweed which come into bloom at about the time that they
are feeding their second brood.

Wild arum (lords and ladies or cuckoo pint): A flower, B sectioned flower,
C fruit

It was while photographing one of our most fascinating hedgerow
plants, lords and ladies, that I was privileged to disturb one of the
most intriguing of British mammals, the hedgehog. There in the hedge
bottom a female was suckling two young beneath the shade of a
butterbur leaf. She blinked as I moved the leaf and allowed the bright
sun to penetrate through to the ground where she lay. I replaced the
protective leaf and to my surprise Mrs Hedgehog continued to suckle.

Foxglove

Hedgehogs

With a common species, it is easy to think we understand everything about it until we try to write down what we know. With the hedgehog, a typical hedge-bottom dweller, it would take longer to write out a list of so far unanswered questions than to record positive facts. The following was published in the *Sunday Express* (12 August 1979):

Soviet veterinary experts are investigating the case of a hedgehog which travelled 48 miles to return to the home where it had been cared for.

The story of Topa is told in the Soviet newspaper *Radyanska Ukraina*. Topa, its paw broken, was found on a country road by Nadezhda Ushakova, a doctor at Donetsk hospital.

She took it home, set the paw and cared for the animal until it was fit. Then she gave Topa to her grand-daughter who took it to her home in the town of Dimitrov, 48 miles away. Soon afterwards, Dr. Ushakova received a letter from her grand-daughter saying that Topa had refused to eat and had become very sluggish, so she had taken it to the forest and set it free.

Two months later Dr. Ushakova returned home from work and found Topa sitting on her doorstep. Now Topa is staying with the doctor and veterinary scientists are trying to discover more about the homing instincts of hedgehogs.

This delightful story should at least stop us from being surprised that the hedgehog finds its way home after a night out in search of food. Its original habitat was the ancient forest, although not pine woods because of the shortage of insects in the leaf-litter. It quickly adapted to the woodland edge with the woodland taken away — yet another definition of a hedge. Hedgehog bones from the Miocene period, some 25 million years ago, have been identified from fossil remains, but for written records we must go back to Anglo-Saxon times when the animal was called *il*, a diminutive of *igel*, its present-day German name. In Norman-French the name was *herichun*, which could have evolved into the English name of 'urchin'. It was not until the middle of the fifteenth century that 'hedgehog' was first used and not until the eighteenth that it became general. It is more than likely that the change in name for the animal reflected the increase in the number of hedges.

The hedgehog has frequently found itself at odds with countryfolk and several of the accusations against it should be carefully examined. Does it suck eggs? Does it 'steal' milk from cows? Does it carry away fruit impaled upon its spines? Is it immune from poisons? All these stories were thought to be true in the Middle Ages and as late as 1564 an Act of Parliament placed a price on the head of the hedgehog; a glance through churchwardens' accounts shows that quite large sums could be obtained by those who cleared the area of these egg-sucking, milk-drinking, fruit-stealing, almost immortal, verminous mammals. The dawn of the scientific age brought a total rejection of all four suggestions, which were thought to be the ravings of unbalanced bumpkins. But in an age of scientific observation we have had cause to think again. There is some evidence that a few individuals do take and suck eggs, though not very often. Any scavenging urchin finding a broken egg will lap it up with glee, and it is easy to see how the careless poultry-keeper could blame a hedgehog for his own clumsiness. Sucking milk from a cow's udder? Just after dawn in a Lakeland meadow I observed a cow lying at ease, cudding gently. As I approached she stood up and made her way uphill towards a stone wall. Where she had been lying the grass was white with milk which had obviously been leaking from her udder. There was a hedgehog — ever the opportunist — lapping up the splashings. I have often recalled this in the light of recent debates. There is one piece of significant scientific evidence available: sucking is a reflex action which most mammals only possess during the period when they are actually being fed by their mother; hedgehogs, however, retain this sucking reflex throughout their life!

Equally fascinating is the old story of the relationship between the hedgehog and fruit. Frances Pitt in her book *Wild Animals in Britain*, published in 1939, says 'It is perhaps a pity to spoil a good yarn by

'Hedgehog-lore'

mentioning that a hedgehog is not a vegetarian and never looks at
fruit.' I confess to being a Frances Pitt fan, but on this occasion I am
sure she is wrong. Hedgehogs are insectivores — their staple diet
consists of invertebrates — but being opportunist feeders they will eat

fruits on occasion, especially when over-ripe. Doubtless hedgehogs have been seen walking around with fruit accidentally stuck to their spines, and this is how the idea of the animal being its own 'mobile larder' may have arisen. The lengths to which the hedgehog will go in order to secure a meal in fact seem to have few limits, since even the venomous adder is included in its menu. That leads us to the fourth controversial question — 'Is the hedgehog immune to poisons?' The answer to this question seems to be 'yes' — at least when compared with some animals, including man himself. It appears to consume large numbers of bees and wasps with little harm, it is 7,000 times more resistant to tetanus than we are, and large doses of arsenic, cyanide, morphine and strychnine are needed to overcome it. There is an oft-repeated story of one individual lapping up car-battery acid without any apparent discomfort. The hedgehog will sometimes seek out an adder, spar with it and kill it; occasionally the snake will sink a fang into its attacker, but despite its small body size the hedgehog does not always perish from the effects of the venom. Its usual reaction is to head for the nearest water and drink copiously, then fall asleep, sometimes for up to a week. Death can result but instances of recovery have actually been recorded. Such powers of resistance are remarkable for such a small animal.

Yet another remarkable piece of behaviour demonstrated by this flea-covered ball of spines is a phenomenon now referred to as 'self-anointing'. When a hedgehog approaches a smelly object it salivates excitedly, licks the liquid into a foam and smears this on to its spines. There was no clue to the function of this peculiar pattern of behaviour until recent work at Adelphi University, New York, by Dr Edmund Brodie. Presented with a toad, the hedgehog frothed over the skin and eventually skinned the toad, at the same time rubbing the soapy-looking poison from the toad's skin, to which again it was obviously immune, over its own spines. Brodie maintains, quite rightly I think, that the hedgehog was making use of the toad's poisons to make its own spines yet more of a deterrent to possible predators. Brodie tested this theory by jabbing himself and his willing(?) students with normal and toady spines, finding the latter had a much more unpleasant effect.

The complexities of hedgehog behaviour are considerable. Its method of hibernating has been the subject of much research in recent years. What is obvious is that hibernation is not nearly so prolonged as was previously suggested, and the statement still found in many publications that the animal goes to sleep in October and awakens quite suddenly in April is simply not true. Food shortage and falling temperature have both been suggested as factors initiating hibernation, but it has now been established beyond doubt that it is the shortening length of daylight which determines the onset.

Two hedgerow butterflies: cabbage white (opposite) and peacock (above)

Towards the end of summer the animal develops an almost insatiable appetite and its fat deposits build up quickly. This fat is of two types. The normal white fat builds up around body organs and beneath the skin, making the first reserves to be drawn upon during the period of inactivity. Brown fat has been discovered in the region of thorax and shoulder and tests have shown this to have a higher calorific value than white fat. The accumulated brown fat is kept until all the white-fat deposits have been drawn upon, and has been named the hibernating gland. It is, however, found also in animals which do not hibernate — the newly born human infant, for example. It is crucial for the survival of the hibernating hedgehog. For once folklore and scientific observation are more or less in agreement. Gypsies who eat hedgehogs say that there are two distinct types of animal — which they call beef hedgehogs (those with brown fat?) and mutton hedgehogs (those with white fat?).

In addition to laying up a reserve food supply, any successful hibernator must cut down its use of energy dramatically. During hibernation the body temperature falls from 37 °C to as low as 4 °C, but if it goes even lower the animal wakes up. It shivers, which rubs the tissues together and generates heat by friction, just as rubbing our hands together does. The hedgehog then tries to find some food and then a warmer place before going to sleep again. Thus hibernation is not a period of total sleep; this is why hedgehogs may be seen scavenging in gardens and hedgerows during spells of very low temperatures.

They are not the only creatures moving about in the hedgerows during winter, for the majority of small mammals do not hibernate and they are often easier to observe when the herbaceous vegetation has died down.

Protecting our Hedges

To halt the destruction of the hedges on which so many creatures are dependent is a matter of urgency. Once again compromise has to be the best approach if the needs of modern agriculture and wildlife are both to be met. The Council for the Protection of Rural England produced a report in 1975 which included a three-point plan to allow the public some chance to determine the future of our threatened countryside:

1 There should be some system of notification whereby those planning to remove landscape features such as hedges would have to give notice to the local authority of their intentions.

2 Encouragement should be given to landowners to conserve valuable habitat. Education has its part to play here, but financial inducements will obviously have most effect. Some form of tax relief could be the answer.

3 The third point is by far the most controversial, but it must surely be implemented some time in the future: that in the last resort, local authorities should have the power to prevent removal of habitat considered to be vital.

This three-point plan would give our hedgerow wildlife more of a chance to survive, a chance to which all living organisms are entitled. It is the duty of all of us to conserve these valuable wildlife sanctuaries for posterity.

4
Fields and Farms

The chemicals used on hedgerows have obviously been applied to fields, which are affected by many of the problems discussed in the last chapter. In recent years fields have become very 'clean' as a result of chemical agriculture and this has been much to the detriment of the wild fauna and flora. The most conspicuous effect has been elimination of wild flowers such as self-heal, buttercups, daisies and cowslips from pasture land, whilst from arable areas we have often lost poppies, charlock and corn marigolds. The subtler disappearance of weed seeds and invertebrates such as beetles and spiders has had profound effects upon birds; the grey partridge, for instance, has widely declined as a result of these disruptions in its food chain. The hatching chicks have a much more frugal choice of food than previously: fewer seeds, fewer sawflies (ploughing decimates the overwintering larvae — they were safe in the fallow winter fields when undersown leys were the practice), and greater dependence upon aphids, whose numbers are fickle, depending upon the spring temperature. Reduction in keepering has also allowed greater predator pressure on the partridge and on other birds of the field, both adults and chicks; weasels, stoats and foxes have increased so significantly as to alter the ecological balance of our fields.

The origin of the first field is easy to define and impossible to date. It came into existence the moment a clearing was made in a forest in order to keep livestock or grow a crop. The difference between prehistoric fields and their modern counterparts is really one of permanence. All that the fields of Stone Age man did, all he required them to do, was to keep his stock alive and protect it from wild beasts until he wished to move on — literally to pastures new. This nomadic existence was general till about 1000 BC, when we have the first evidence of permanent farmsteads. Even the more permanent settlers, however, lived in what amounted to transient hovels, which were quickly abandoned when the soil became drained of its nutrients by having to grow a succession of crops without the benefit of

Mowing the hay, Padiham, Nr. Burnley

intermittent fertiliser. No sooner had the fields been abandoned than nature began to reclaim her own. Wild grasses, such as purple moor grass and sheep's fescue, would have been amongst the first to gain a foothold, followed soon by the various species of bent. These would gradually render the ground fertile once more and in would come birch, hazel, ash and finally oak. Thus the scar would heal.

The Romans did much to improve the agricultural efficiency of Britain during their 350-year occupation, and it has been suggested that they brought some four million acres under cultivation. When they abandoned these islands much hard-won agricultural land returned to wilderness and was not tamed again until the Saxons came with their oxen-drawn ploughs and communal open-field system. This neat, compact design for living involved a number of dwellings surrounded by large open fields in which people laboured. Each house was in fact a farmhouse, but a farmhouse with a difference. The farmers were only allowed to keep body and soul together, the land itself and the profits accruing therefrom belonging to the chief. Great advances were made in agricultural techniques; for the first time man in Britain realised that he could keep a few animals safe and fed during the winter without going through the wasteful ritual of the autumn

Wraysholme Tower Farm, near Arnside, Cumbria

slaughter of valuable stock. Here then was organised farming, around the fertile field — but a field with few hedges, apart from those separating the land of one settlement from the next.

The value of careful husbandry and adequate fertilising of the land was not suddenly understood, however, and during the early Norman period most of the manorial in-fighting was over some particularly fertile area of land equidistant between two and sometimes three manors. It has been suggested that during the thirteenth century the population of Britain, England especially, had become too large to be supported by the agricultural endeavours of the time. Thus by the time of the arrival of the Black Death in 1349 many among the population were already weakened by hunger and succumbed to the disease all the more easily. Traditionally, as seen in Chapter 3, it has been believed that the Black Death caused a switch from arable farming to sheep farming. Some historians, however, feel that the trend away from arable to pastoral farming came rather later. One supporter of this theory, Philip Zeigler, agrees that the switch from labour-intensive crops to sheep was a logical consequence of a fall in population, but he goes on:

Because something could reasonably be expected to have happened, it

Wood clearing near Okehampton, Devon

does not follow that it did. In fact, there is little evidence to show that there was any movement to pasture farming, and none to show that the movement was general throughout the country. The acreage under plough certainly dropped but this was no more than a symptom of the retreat from the less profitable marginal lands which was already marked before the plague. There is no corresponding increase in wool production to set against this trend.

Thus Zeigler argues that the swing to sheep came later. It was certainly evident during Tudor times. During the reigns of Henry VIII and especially Elizabeth I, two interesting complaints were being registered: the rapid destruction of native woodlands — discussed in Chapter 1 — and that insufficient care was being taken of the grazing land. We see time and time again throughout history that a problem must be openly recognised before a solution can be devised. From Tudor times the profession of the grazier become more and more important and money could be accumulated by advising panic-stricken landowners how to prevent their fields from becoming infertile deserts.

The value of wheat was realised and 'yield per acre' was by now a phrase on every farmer's lips. Necessity may be the mother of

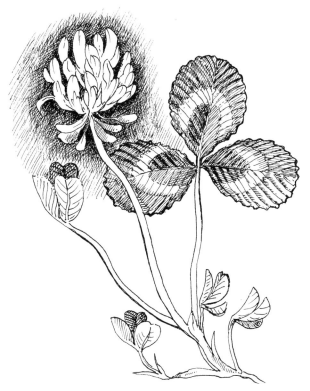

Clover

invention, but it can probably spawn another offspring, close observation. It was noticed that old fields which had been used to enclose cattle and sheep, and so had been manured, retained their fertility. Now we had mixed farming and the first hint of the value of 'rotation'. One further development completed the picture of the English farm which has lasted almost to the present day. Andrew Tarranton wrote a very significant book in 1653, *The Great Improvement of Lands by Clover*, pointing out that land on which clover had been grown was richer in consequence. He did not know why, but his method worked, which was all that mattered.

Whenever a crop is harvested the essential nitrates obtained from the soil are removed with it. The next crop of plants will therefore have fewer nitrates on which to feed and eventually the crop will fail. Clover, and often plants belonging to the leguminosae family, which includes peas, beans and gorse, has nodules on its roots which contain certain bacteria that can convert atmospheric nitrogen (78 per cent of the air consists of nitrogen) into nitrates which another plant can use. It was realised that if clover was grown every four years and ploughed into the ground the fertility of the field could be restored. Here then is the

Sheep in winter at Chipping near Preston

basis of the crop-rotation system which dominated our agriculture for so long. How often have you seen a field of clover and heard it described as grass?

All Flesh is Grass

The grass family, the Graminae, embraces a huge and highly specialised range of species. Mankind has found more uses for grasses than for any other plant family, and that's saying something. Wheat, oats, barley, spring immediately to mind, but others have been used to yield sugar, starch and aromatic oils and for thatching dwellings. Where would the Scots be without whisky and porridge? A look at a food pyramid for a field indicates the basic part played by grasses in our economy.

In Britain we have over 150 species of grass growing wild, more than in any other family of flowering plants. Sometimes the flowers of grasses are so small that a magnifying glass is needed to see their detail; because their pollen is carried by wind and not by insects, they do not need to advertise their presence by large brightly coloured

A selection of grasses: (left to right) sheep's fescue, quaking grass, meadow foxtail, marram, silver hair, sand catstail

petals and sepals. The male anthers and the female stigmas are surrounded by three types of modified leaf, the glume, lemma and palea, which protect the ripening seed — in cereals known as the corn.

Life under the Grass

Most of the inhabitants of present-day fields originated as woodland animals. Many burrowing animals found it easier to make headway through soil broken up by the plough than to thrust through masses of roots. Any discussion of life in the soil must take account of two species in particular, namely the earthworm and the mole. Without earthworms, our soil — and consequently our countryside — would be much the poorer. Up to 3 million worms may occupy every acre of

113

Food pyramid for a field, with grass at the bottom

grass, each an organic plough, churning, mixing, digesting and aerating the soil, constantly casting it up to the surface. By pulling leaves into the ground for fodder they also create a natural compost. And if earthworms are vital to the good heart of the soil, the agents that disrupt their labours are also influential: earthworms are eaten by hedgehogs, badgers, even by foxes and tawny owls among others, but no account of their life history would be complete without mentioning the mole — their arch enemy but still a possible asset to the soil in its own right.

The earthworm is indeed a most underrated beast. Many people, among them otherwise knowledgeable naturalists, think that an earthworm is an earthworm and that's it. In Europe there are over 220 species, of which 25 are found in Britain; only about 10, however, can be described as common, and they are well worth the trouble of getting to know.

The most frequently described species is *Lumbricus terrestris* and

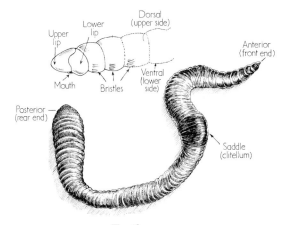

Earthworm

like all species it finds the top foot of soil (30cm or so) much more to its liking than the deeper layers, although it burrows to lower levels in very hot or cold weather. Two other species are of particular interest since these are more active in winter than in summer: these have no vernacular names and are known scientifically as *Allolobophora longa* and *Allolobophora nocturna*. During hot, dry summer months they 'hibernate' deep in the soil. Since the word hibernate is usually reserved for sleep in winter this behaviour has been termed diapause.

Ask anyone to name a few famous naturalists and I would guess that the names of Gilbert White and Charles Darwin would spring up. Neither of them thought mere worms beneath their dignity, and they watched them with great interest. White, writing in 1777, notes:

> Gardeners and farmers express their detestation of worms, the former because they render their walks unsightly, and make them much work; and the latter because, as they think, worms eat their green corn. But these men would find that the earth without worms would soon become cold, hardbound, and void of fermentation; and consequently sterile...Worms seem to be the great promotors of vegetation, which would proceed but lamely without them, by boring, perforating and loosening the soil and rendering it pervious to rains and the fibres of plants by drawing straws, and stalks of leaves and twigs into it; and most of all, by throwing up such infinite numbers of lumps of earth called worm-casts which being their excrement, is a fine manure for grain and grass.

Darwin wrote loftily in the 1830s of the splendours of the Galapagos Islands and, with Wallace, set before the Linnaean Society in 1858 his theory of evolution which rocked the civilised world, redirecting the whole of its biological thinking. He then seemed to look down at the microcosm of life rather than soar to loftier heights. In 1881 he published the results of his deliberations on worms, 'The Formation of Vegetable Mould Through the Action of Worms with Observations of

Starling — another species which has learnt to follow the plough

Their Habits'. In this he commented: 'It may be doubted whether there are any other animals which have played such an important part in the history of the world as these lowly organised creatures.'

Darwin's interest in earthworms was by no means a transient thing and his observations stretched over a period of more than 30 years! He estimated that the worms living in one acre of land would produce 10 tons of casts in one year. From this and similar data he estimated that solid objects would gradually be buried as a consequence of this activity and would disappear at the rate of about 0.2 inches (50mm) per year. Modern workers think this figure is slightly too high but do not disagree with the basic premise.

Whilst it must be admitted that forest clearance probably benefited earthworms, ploughing on occasion can be regarded as a disadvantage to some species since it makes the entry to the soil much easier for predators. One has only to watch the hordes of birds following the plough — rooks and black-headed gulls prominent among them — to realise this. The delightful robin sitting on the gardener's fence realises that disturbed soil means easy pickings. Pasture land seems therefore to be the ideal habitat and this has been borne out by the

Robin

work of the Danish scientists who have calculated that the weight of earthworms on pasture land may well be greater than the stock grazing on it.

The pasture land, however, also provides sanctuary for the mole, a more lethal enemy to worms than any bird. Statistics can be used to prove anything, and it can in fact be shown that the mole is Britain's most dangerous animal! Look at this evidence:

It is hinted that in 1100 William Rufus died when his horse fell over a molehill and threw him. The story of the arrow may have been invented in order that a prince of the realm could be said to have died as befitted a warrior.

Then in 1702 King William III's horse did stumble over a molehill and threw its rider with fatal consequences. This gave rise to the now famous Jacobite toast 'To the Little Gentleman in Black Velvet'. No other wild animal has so decimated our royal hierarchy!

The many vernacular names for the mole include the middle-English *molle* from which we derive the present-day name. It is thought that molle is a diminutive of mouldiwarp, an Old English word that literally

117

Mole

translates as *molde*, earth, and *werpen*, to throw. Hence we have the earth-thrower, a much more meaningful name than *Talpa europaea* Linnaeus. Nothing is designed to anger the farmer or gardener more than a line of molehills, and it is always assumed that this means damaged land. Is this fair? Of all the mammals of Britain the mole is perhaps the most difficult to assess. Certainly there is good to be said about it, since its burrowing activities, like those of the earthworms, allow air to diffuse more easily into the soil and must improve drainage. It is therefore difficult to sympathise with the wholesale persecution of the beautiful mole which has been part of our country scene for centuries. A law of 1566 made it obligatory to kill vermin and a glance at churchwardens' accounts will bear ample witness. 'Moles were persistently persecuted (more than 2,000 were killed in May 1674) and for them ½d each was paid; here again dialect names were sometimes used: 1664 May 24 "paid for taking five dozen and four mouldy warps £00.02.03". In 1673 June 2 "paid for 2 dozen and a half of moulds from Ancoats £00.01.03".' This information, quoted from A. W.

Boyd's *Country Diary of a Cheshire Man* (1945), was abstracted from the churchwardens' accounts for Manchester, between 1664 and 1711, which are housed in the Rylands Library. Similar records could be obtained from most areas of the country. To the skilful countryman here was a lucrative source of income and the mole-catcher was a regular feature of the countryside. He is beautifully described in 'The Mole Catcher' by John Clare (1793–1864).

> When melted snow leaves bare the black-green rings
> And grass begins in freshening hues to shoot,
> When thawing dirt to shoes of ploughmen clings,
> And silk-haired moles get liberty to root,
> An ancient man goes plodding round the fields
> Which solitude seems claiming as her own,
> Wrapt in greatcoat that from tempest shields
> Patched thick with every colour but its own.
>
> With spuds and traps and horsehair string supplied
> He potters out to seek each fresh-made hill;
> Pricking the greensward where they love to hide
> He sets his treacherous snares, resolved to kill,
> And on the willow sticks bent to the grass,
> That such as touched jerk up in bouncing springs,
> Soon as the little hermit tries to pass
> His little carcass on the gibbet hings.
>
> And as a triumph to his matchless skill
> On some grey willow where a road runs by
> That passers may behold his power to kill
> On the bough's twigs he'll many a felon tie;
> On every common dozens may be met
> Dangling on bent twigs bleaching to the sun
> Whose melancholy fates meet no regret
> Though dreamless of the snare they could not shun.
>
> On moors and commons and the pasture green
> He leaves them undisturbed to root and run.
> Enlarging hills that have for ages been
> Basking in mossy swellings to the sun.
> The pismies too their tip-tops yearly climb
> To lay their eggs and hunt the shepherd's crumbs
> Never disturbed save when for summer thyme
> The trampling sheep upon their dwelling comes.

In recent years, work by several zoologists has thrown light on the dark world of the mole. When you are lucky enough to see a living mole — far less often seen than its hillocks! — your first impression of this busy tunnelling machine will be its tiny size. Moles measure just over 5¾in (140mm) with the females just a little smaller at 5¼in (130mm). The stumpy tail adds a further 1½in (30mm).

Physically the long round body, short close-grained fur and broad

119

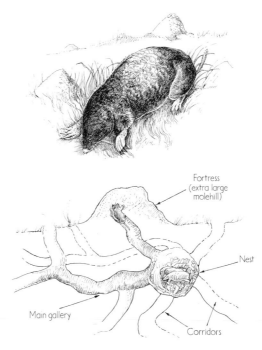

Mole-burrow system

paddle-like forefeet are ideally designed for burrowing. Whichever way you run your hand along the body, the pile of the fur lies flat; this means the animal can just as easily move backwards as forwards through its burrow system, without ruffling its fur. It was probably this velvet-like consistency that made moleskin popular wearing apparel until fairly recently.

The mole has little need of sight and the tiny eyes are almost totally concealed beneath the fur. Each eye is complete with lens, retina, optic nerve and so on, but measures only 1mm across. To compensate for poor vision the senses of smell and hearing are acute. The snout is particularly sensitive, being covered all over by minute papillae, connected by a rich network of nerves to the brain, called eimers organs. When the mole is investigating its surroundings extra blood can be pumped into the snout, causing it to swell and erect the eimers organs. It has been suggested that these are so sensitive they can detect moving air along the burrows, such as that pushed along by an animal advancing towards it — a refined version of the way we detect the approach of a train on a city's underground railway.

Many of the oldtime writers give the impression that moles live together in harmonious family groups beneath our pasturelands. Nothing could be further from the truth. For the most part the sexes live apart and if they do happen to meet they fight ferociously. Even during the breeding season the meeting of two moles will produce fierce shrieks followed immediately by a fight, often to the death. The appetite of the mole is also worthy of note. As an animal living in almost total darkness most of its rhythms are not controlled by daylight and it seems to operate in alternating four-hourly periods of rest and activity. Should it be unable to find food within a few hours it can fail to maintain its high consumption of energy and therefore perish. Moles seem to take no vegetable food at all and so cannot be held responsible for eating farm crops — although in burrowing they may occasionally damage the roots. They do however show a distinct liking for earthworms which, as we have already seen, are of great benefit to the farmer; however to balance this they also eat wireworms and other invertebrates that are serious pests to crops.

Some of the mole's feeding is actually carried out above ground and the 'umpty-tumpt' can sometimes be seen, or more often heard, grubbing about among fallen leaves. Slugs, worms, caterpillars and other invertebrates are all eaten, but it is at this time that the mole itself is at its most vulnerable; its bones have been found in the pellets of birds of prey such as barn owl, tawny owl, and buzzard.

Life in the Grass

Worm and mole are the best-known beasts beneath the field, but what about the beasts *of* the field?

A variety of birds and mammals that have evolved in this country have adapted to our field system, and have made an important impact on the pattern and efficiency of land use (think of how the woodpigeon has kept farmers on the hop ever since they started growing fields of brassicas). The solitary hare is often thought of as an innocuous inhabitant of open fields, but like its social cousin the rabbit, if its numbers are too great it is capable of great damage to agriculture and forestry. Both fall prey to the fox, for which the field system seems to have been almost expressly designed, with its shrubby lairs, hedgerow runs and open ground for the chase. The development of the field system has been somewhat of a mixed blessing for bird life. Some species like the starling, rook and lapwing seem to have been here forever and yet they were formerly confined to Eurasian steppeland and only colonised Britain in large numbers as suitably open tracts of land were created. Others, like the curlew, have more recently successfully invaded arable land, in this case even for breeding, from its native moorland haunts. In modern times the intensive mechanised farming of land and success in eradicating insects and weed seeds (pests to man but food to birds) have had far-reaching effects on many of these colonisers, driving several such as the stone curlew, corncrake and lapwing in diminishing numbers back to marginal land, and virtually eliminating some, such as the quail. For other birds, like barn owls and swallows, the farm buildings themselves have been an important resource, providing nooks and crannies for nests. The introduction of creviceless, factory-made barns has proved a setback to both these attractive farmland birds.

If we look at a selection of farmland species we come to understand their part in our countryside fabric.

A somewhat unusual occurrence has, of recent years, come into being in the month of September; this is now known as the Festival of the Hare. For four weeks from as far away as Stowe, Eton, Clifton, Cambridge and Dumfries people gather together in the county to celebrate the hunting of the hare. The county of Northumberland, now shorn of Tyneside, largely consists of agricultural land with a few coal mines in its south-eastern region. There is also the vast forest of Kielder, the largest man-created forest area in Western Europe. These conditions appear to favour a scattered hare population. The festival has not come into being suddenly; for many years universities and public school packs have hunted in the county before their various terms began. During the month of September most country inns and hotels are booked solid and it is now quite usual for the visiting sportsmen to book a year in advance. Flesh for hounds is generously supplied by the many fox hound packs in the county. Kennelling hounds appears to be no great problem for the beagles seem to thrive in quite moderate quarters. The host pack is the old Newcastle and District Beagles whose joint masters have a great deal to do before the Festival of the Hare in fixing meets, arranging suitable accommodation for hunt personnel and hounds for the hunting fraternity and particularly the beagling enthusiasts; this has now become a four week period not to be missed.

This quotation reads as if it could have come out of an eighteenth-century newspaper, but it is actually a piece from *The Guardian*'s Country Diary of 12 October 1979. Too much sentiment should be avoided, and shooting a hare — and enjoying it jugged — when the local hare population is damaging crops is rational enough. Hare coursing is another matter: here it is the means of destruction that many of us detest.

The hare in fact must be well used to being hunted, as our forebears killed it out of positive fear rather than for fun. The sight of a white hare was amongst the omens of death (others equally portentous being a butterfly seen at night and molehills encircling a house). This type of fear of the unknown was worldwide, but the idea of witches having familiars or animals with which they could communicate seems to have been generated in Britain. It was firmly believed that some witches could transform themselves into hares, and having done this proceed to suck milk from cows. The pursuit of witches was particularly vigorous in Scotland and in the Pendleside district of East

Hare

Lancashire. In Scotland especially it was not uncommon for extreme and humiliating torture to be used in order to get a frightened girl or aged crone to admit to being a witch. The confession extracted from Isabel Gowrie in the year 1662 has to be viewed with sympathy for the 'witch' herself. She admitted that she could transform herself into a hare by reciting a special spell: 'I shall go intill a hare, with sorrow and sych and meikle care; and I shall go in the Devil's name, Ay while I come home again.' To change back she repeated 'Hare, hare, God send thee care. I am in a Hare's likeness now, But I shall be in a woman's likeness even now.' The only way to kill a witch-hare was to shoot her/it with a silver bullet.

The law relating to shooting hares, however, is anomalous. Under the Ground Game Act 1880, a landowner or his agent can kill and sell hares, but only to a person licensed to deal in game. Although there is no official close season, hares may not be offered for sale between

1 March and 31 July. If the original object of this restriction was to give the species a trouble-free breeding season, it is only partially successful; I have found young hares (leverets) as early as 17 February and as late as 8 November. Indeed as I write this chapter on 4 November, I have just been told of a leveret released into the wild after being bottle-fed during early October.

The hare is not only much larger than the rabbit, but its ears are also much longer in proportion and black-tipped, and its long back legs make it one of the swiftest of all wild animals, especially when running uphill. Although they prefer not to enter water, hares can swim well enough. Indeed their behaviour gives the impression of a mixture of astuteness and stupidity — probably accentuated by their wide-set eyes which can see everything to the side and also most of what is going on behind, yet often fail to take in what is straight in front of them — a fact which has long been known to poachers, who approach hares head-on. The antics of a courting hare in March are notorious; Andrew Young's 'March Hares' is one onlooker's account.

> I made myself as a tree,
> No withered leaf twirling on me;
> No, not a bird that stirred my boughs,
> As looking out from wizard brows
> I watched those lithe and lovely forms
> That raised the leaves in storms.
>
> I watched them leap and run,
> Their bodies hollowed in the sun
> To thin transparency,
> That I could clearly see
> The shallow colour of their blood
> Joyous in love's full flood.
>
> I was content enough
> Watching that serious game of love,
> That happy hunting in the wood
> Where the pursuer was the more pursued,
> To stand in breathless hush
> With no more life myself than tree or bush

The origin of the scientific name for the rabbit, *Oryctolagus cuniculus*, is interesting. *Oryctolagus* has Greek roots: *orukter* is a tool for digging, *logos* a hare, and so we have a 'digging hare'. *Cuniculus*, of Latin origin, is an underground passage.

There has always been argument over when the rabbit appeared in Britain. Fossil remains of mammals having a similar (not identical) structure to modern rabbits have been found in rocks aged 10,000 to 15,000 years and belonging to a period geologists define as the Pleistocene. No mention is made of the rabbit in the Domesday Book

Rabbit

of 1086 but it does merit entry in chronicles from the twelfth century onwards. Some writers have suggested that the Romans introduced it, quoting as evidence that they were eaten by the upper classes, being considered a delicacy. Indeed they were held in enough esteem to be used to decorate the face of coins in use during the reign of the Emperor Hadrian (AD 117–138). This man built us our famous wall: did he also bring us the rabbit? H. N. Southern, one of the authors of *The Handbook of British Mammals*, tells me that all reliable evidence indicates that the rabbit was introduced by the Normans. The surprising thing to us is that rabbits were for a long time so uncommon that they were only eaten at special feasts such as coronations. The meat was known to be nutritious as well as tasty, a fact supported by analysis, which reveals a higher proportion of protein than in any other form of flesh. The valuable stock was cosseted and protected by a warrener. The population of rabbits must have risen considerably by the eighteenth century, and a higher proportion of the human population was allowed to eat the meat and use the fur for clothing. The poor were still not included, however, and anyone caught 'poaching rabbits by night' was liable to seven years' transportation!

During the Industrial Revolution many of the traditional jobs done by country people were deserted in favour of the higher wages to be earned in expanding towns. Rabbits from enclosures escaped, the hunting pressure was less and the population of the beast rose sharply. It was only in the year 1954, however, that rabbits were officially declared a pest; it was then estimated that they were eating £60 millions worth of crops each year. Drastic action was justified. Myxomatosis then appeared (or was it introduced from France deliberately?), and was an immediate solution to the problem. In the first year after the disease appeared agricultural production rose by between 15 and 20 per cent.

The myxomatosis virus can cause almost 100 per cent mortality in some populations of rabbits. It seems to affect no other species, except very occasionally a hare, and it is carried from one rabbit to another by an insect, in the case of the British rabbit by the flea *Silopsyllus cuniculi*. To quote *The Sunday Times* of 9 January 1977:

> When myxomatosis arrived in Britain, Dr (Miriam) Rothschild was asked by the Government to discover if fleas were the vector of the virus. Proving that the fleas spread the disease was, she says 'as easy as falling off a log' but then she turned to the far more difficult problem of trying to breed the vector flea in captivity.
>
> No one had tried to do it before. Solving the problem was rather like a detective story and in the end 'we managed to show that it was the sex hormones of the rabbit that controlled the breeding of the flea and that it would only breed on pregnant does. Once having established that, you could spray the appropriate hormone on the outside of the flea and get it to breed without a pregnant rabbit...' Dr Rothschild has no hesitation in justifying its use: 'When you see a whole country devastated by a pest you realise that it is you or the rabbit.'

She has a point — as well as laboratory expertise — yet this is not the only viewpoint. If you have a surfeit of one of the richest supplies of protein in the world could you not eat it, or export it to someone who

A week-old rabbit rescued from a hungry ferret, being hand fed

could? If you could not sell it, why not give it away, rather than investing in machines to cultivate crops which actually provide *less* protein? Maybe it would be worth rethinking the rabbit question, for there is mounting evidence that rabbits are actually becoming immune to the virus and are growing bigger than ever before. Beautiful bouncing bunnies now grace our countryside; fewer die with stinking pus-filled eyes and ears and swollen heads. Do we need to develop another deadly virus or could we not focus our intelligence on the problem and expect our local chippie to offer rabbit and chips?

The fox belongs to our countryside, though I seriously wondered whether to include it in the discussion of urban wildlife. One piece of evidence supporting the latter course was my own observation. I had been out to dinner in Manchester and was returning along Deansgate (quite sober!), when a fox crossed the road in front of my car, stopped near Kendal's store and then trotted away. A second was furnished by the introduction by Colin Willock to Brian Vesey-Fitzgerald's book *Town Fox Country Fox.*

> To many city-dwellers and not a few countrymen the idea of seeing a fox three miles from Piccadilly Circus may seem utterly absurd, but I assure you I have done so on many occasions. Once, at three a.m. in the Spaniard's Road, near Hampstead Heath, I saw and heard a dustbin lid fall and immediately assumed the cause to be a scavenging cat. But the raider was a dog fox, a shade seedy of coat perhaps, but certainly not undernourished. All the foxes that I saw along the heath seemed to be living most handsomely in their unlikely habitat.

But the fox (*Vulpes vulpes*) must have originated as a woodland animal and learned to exist close to man's habitation. There is evidence that foxes can climb trees and some spend a lot of time sleeping in arboreal dens. The majority of foxes never kill any domestic animal and may live close to us without our being aware of their presence; they are commoner than we often imagine. That is not to say that the farmer is wrong to fear the fox, because some rogue individuals do untold damage to domestic stock and have to be removed, even by hunting if need be.

Fox hunting in Britain takes two distinct forms, the familiar hunting on horseback and hunting on foot over the Northern fells, which are unsuitable for horses. The former is a ritualised form of entertainment, with many rules to be obeyed. The red-coated Master of Foxhounds is in charge of the hunt, a pack of bitch hounds, and pays its expenses, often largely out of his own pocket. There is often a professional, sometimes highly skilled, Huntsman who can be blamed if no fox is killed, and who is in control of a pack of dog-hounds: there

127

Fox

are professional whippers-in and kennel staff. So the hobby is expensive. In contrast the North Country hunts are rougher affairs. The huntsmen wear grey, not red — 'Do ye ken John Peel, With his coat so grey?' The fox is hunted up hill and down dale, and by the time it is killed, the hunters are too tired to do much else but sleep — at least the hounds are! Personally I have more sympathy with fox hunters, for example, than with hare coursers. Hunts kill some 15,000 foxes a year, and without them other forms of destruction would have to be used, potentially more unpleasant for the fox than what is usually a relatively swift kill by the hunt. When serious damage is done to man's enterprises, one has to be realistic about the need to keep down fox numbers. Enthusiasts often state, too, that without the hunt, with all its colourful trappings, Reynard would soon become extinct in Britain; and both sides of the argument want to avoid that! Hunts, of course, are easy prey for critics; they have been known to import continental foxes to ensure that there is something for them to chase; they have occasionally suggested that the fox enjoys being hunted — a nonsense if ever there was one.

Hunting on horseback — Pendle Forest Hunt, Downham, near Clitheroe

The fox will survive as long as man throws scraps into his dustbins and bones on to his rubbish dump. He is that sort of animal.

William MacGillivray writing in 1840 recorded that the landrail — as the corncrake was often called — arrives from North Africa in the beginning of summer and departs early in September: 'It is generally distributed, occurring in abundance in the most northern parts of Scotland and its islands.' This corresponds to its present status in Scotland. In England and Wales the population has dwindled, a decline thought by most ornithologists to have begun in the nineteenth century with the advent of mechanised cutting of the grass crops, amongst which the landrail nests. In the old days the farm worker with his scythe would notice the nest and the majority were humane enough to leave it intact. Only at the last possible moment would the bird rise with a crack of wings and fly, legs dangling, to a safer spot. Modern farm machinery moves much more quickly and the driver will not even notice the birds and nests. A corncrake escaping in a panic too often strikes overhead power lines, which are responsible for the deaths of many birds, especially wildfowl and rails.

Hunting on foot — Windermere Harriers at Wrynose Pass, Cumbria

All is thought to look black on the horizon of the corncrake as the clouds of extinction gather. I would however point firmly not to one but to two silver linings. The British Trust for Ornithology carried out a survey, for their *Atlas*, of all Britain's breeding birds between 1968 and 1972. From data received, a population of around 6,000 breeding pairs of corncrakes was estimated, a figure nowhere nearly low enough to postulate immediate extinction. The Scottish and Irish populations seem almost as high as ever, and the bird is also still present and breeding, even if in low densities, in most counties of England and Wales, even those heavily committed to competitive agriculture. It is, however, now considered rare enough to be afforded special protection in Great Britain under Schedule I of the Protection of Birds Acts 1954–67.

There is another even more hopeful sign. Writers have been commenting for centuries upon the tendency of the corncrake population to fluctuate from a period of scarcity to one of great abundance, a situation which is also noticed amongst many migratory birds. Similar trends can also be seen in mammals like the lemming, or

Corncrake

even our own red squirrel. Our lifespan is not long enough to allow us to arrive at a balanced view. For this reason, if for no other, the writings of old-time natural historians need to be regularly consulted, so long as it is remembered that their records may have a 'local' bias. William Turner writing in 1544, Francis Willoughby in 1678 and Montagu in 1802 are agreed that the corncrake was common in the north and west but rare in the south. Gilbert White points out that the corncrake was a bit of a rarity in Hampshire: 'A man brought me a landrail or Daker-hen, a bird so rare in this district that we seldom see more than one in a season, and these only in Autumn.' A possible reason for the decrease in corncrake numbers may have been that the increased efficiency in farming techniques was rendering the earth more fertile so that crops were being grown on what had been waste land. This has now been followed by developments which enable the crops to be ripened earlier and cut closer and this has returned the corncrake (despite the evolution in some places of an appropriately earlier breeding season) to its original position as a resident. Once more in regions of the country where the traditional methods of haymaking remain largely unchanged the wheel of nature has turned full circle.

I once had the privilege of walking the fields with a retired Scots blacksmith. David was then well into his eighties, but one of the most competent naturalists I have met. He always ceremoniously raised his cap to the first snowdrop of the year and the first swallow.

'You should always,' he said, 'salute the first signs of spring.' Ever since I raise my own hat to the bird which to my mind is the harbinger of spring to the British field — the curlew (*Numenius arquata*). David called the species by the old name of whaup, and it also had another vernacular name, whitterick. Its bubbling, rippling, gurgling flight call seems to signal its joy on returning to the breeding fields after having spent the winter months along the coasts, where temperatures were a little higher. The long down-curved bill is slid deep into mud or earth in search of the invertebrates it eats. At the first sign of lengthening of the days the curlews return to the fields and moors and begin a-courting. It is not only the sound of the bird which gives pleasure to the naturalist. The soaring display flight, skilful if only momentary, is followed by a smooth planing flight towards the earth which is a delight to watch.

In complete contrast to the corncrake the population of the curlew has increased dramatically this century, though the numbers are checked to some extent by hard winters. Large numbers perished, for example, in the winter of 1962–63 and they did not fare too well during 1979 either. I think that we are seeing yet another example of an ever-fluctuating population, whose trends should be assessed only over a period far exceeding the human lifespan. The descriptions 'rare' and 'common' have to be viewed against the background of the past history of the species. The British Trust for Ornithology's *Atlas* gives an estimate of about 50,000 breeding pairs of curlew in Britain.

I sat down to write this section after returning from the fields. Rain had swept down from a grey sky and water squirted from beneath my feet, and I sought shelter beneath a gnarled hawthorn. Lapwings (*Vanellus vanellus*) were falling like autumn leaves onto the sodden earth and were eagerly pulling up earthworms forced to evacuate their flooded burrows. I could almost detect the birds' enjoyment of the meal. Very few birds have completely waterproof feathers and the torrential rain must have soaked them through. Periodically they shook themselves like dogs and then settled down to feed again.

Lapwings, according to some writers, have learned to fool the

Curlew

Lapwing

earthworms into surfacing, even in dry weather. They drum their feet on the earth and this 'pattering' creates vibrations similar to that of rain falling. Many of the modern Handbooks either do not refer to this activity or assume that it is a recently discovered behaviour pattern. Yet Kenneth Spencer, in his monograph *The Lapwing in Britain*, notes that pattering was mentioned by Buffon (1781) and Latham (1785), and was accepted by such eminent nineteenth-century writers as Montagu, Yarrell and Gould. Bishop Mant describes the practice in his poem about the lapwing:

> For now from field or sandy shore
> In congregated crowds they pour
> Bound o'er the land, now here now there,
> Or sport or frolick in the air
> With restless wing or tap the ground
> In hope the oft repeated sound
> May penetrate the shaking mould
> And fright the earthworm from its hold.

Lapwings are not always, however, able to enjoy all the earthworms they find. Often you see a flock dotted with vigilant black-headed or common gulls, ready to harass, and dispossess, any lapwing tugging up a worm.

Lapwing

In Farm Buildings

The traditional farmhouse and its outbuildings would be a poorer place without the welcome presence of the birds which have learned to live with us. Included here are the ubiquitous house sparrow, the chattering house martin and the screaming swifts; and two of the most interesting of our guests, the barn owl and the swallow.

The barn owl is truly cosmopolitan, being found probably in more countries than almost any other of the world's 8,000-plus species. The status of this lovely pale-coloured owl (*Tyto alba*) in Britain is giving rise to concern, although its condition in 1980 was a little better than its 1970 situation. For once, concern has been voiced for some time, from about 1900 in fact. A survey conducted by the RSPB as long ago as 1932 estimated the British population at 12,000 pairs, plus about 1,000 non-breeding birds, giving a total of some 25,000. By the time the BTO *Atlas* survey results were published, the figure had fallen to about 9,000 birds. Four factors were held to be mainly responsible: loss of habitat (especially the disappearance of old stone-walled barns and their wealth of potential nest-sites), human disturbance, severe winters and toxic chemicals. Since the mid 1960s, however, the latter has been restricted and barn owls — whose food is mice and young rats, plus the odd small bird — are recovering a little.

Do owls have 'supernatural' powers? Can they see in the dark? Barn owls have been credited with extraordinary abilities because of their behaviour. Though not a particularly nervous individual, once when I entered a barn looking for bats and a barn owl slipped off its perch on a beam, ghosted its way past me and, uttering an ear-splitting scream, flew out through the door, I was still shaking ten minutes afterwards. There are records of barn owls actually glowing at night, which must be even more nerve-racking. This phenomenon is due to their roosting habits. If pieces of rotting wood lodge in the feathers, the bacteria contained in it exhibit the power of bioluminescence and the eerie blue-green light splutters as the owl flies. One can imagine the effect this would have had on the superstitious medieval mind.

No creature is able to see in total darkness, but then this never occurs in nature, apart from in the depths of caves and beneath deep water. Nocturnal animals have evolved two strategies to cope with life in very dim light. They have either reduced the size and importance of the eyes, and developed more efficient senses of smell, touch and hearing or like the barn owl have enlarged the eyes so that much more light enters; the eye functions just like a 'fast' camera lens. The cells of the retina have also been modified. The eyes of birds, just like those of mammals, contain cells called rods and cones. Rods are stimulated by

Barn owl

weak light and play no part in colour vision. Cones on the other hand need stronger light to stimulate them but they do record colour. In owls large groups of rods are connected to the same nerve path and thus can operate in very low light intensity, at the expense of sacrificing some colour vision. Colour vision, however, is hardly important in a crepuscular or nocturnal animal. Thus the barn owl can glide around in the twilight, faithfully recording all that is going on in the field below it.

No bird on the British list evokes more admiration than the graceful swallow (*Hirundo rustica*). From May to the end of September swallows swoop around our buildings and fields, mouths gaping open to snap up flying insects. The odd bird may occasionally reach us in March and I once watched two birds hawking over the pond in a Northern park on 22 November.

The ability of this species to commute between Britain and Africa is nothing short of miraculous. That birds migrate is not a modern realisation as an extract from the Bible (Jeremiah, 8, vii) shows.

Swallow

Yea, the stork in the heavens knoweth her appointed times, and the turtle dove and the swallow and the crane observe the time of their coming.

Aristotle also mentioned migration, as did the Roman natural historian Pliny the Elder, but both thought that the swallow hibernated. In the 34th book of his monumental work, Pliny states that swallows spend the winter, often totally bereft of their feathers, in some gloomy retreat on the side of a south-facing mountain slope. The migration versus hibernation battle waged back and forth like a tidal system. *Ortus Sanitatis*, published by Johann Wonnecke in 1485, shows an awareness of the phenomenon of migration, but specifically excludes the swallow.

The stork heralds the spring ... They travel across the sea and fly in large numbers to Asia ... [The swallow] seeks mountain peaks when it leaves for the winter and there it is found all bare and without feathers.

Wonnecke had obviously studied his copy of Pliny and copied him faithfully. In 1555 Olaus Magnus provided another view of the thoughts then in vogue.

Several authors ... have described how swallows often fly from one country to another, travelling to a warm climate for the winter months;

138

Swallow feeding its young

but they have not mentioned the denizens of northern regions which are often pulled from the water by fishermen in a large ball. They cling beak to beak, wing to wing, foot to foot, having bound themselves together in the first days of Autumn.

The reason for what appears to be a far-fetched idea can be appreciated. The last view of a departing swallow in autumn is invariably over water in pursuit of food, and the first spring observation is often just the same. So the suggestion that they spend the winter beneath water had the grudging support of the Rev Gilbert White and of the great Linnaeus himself.

The age of careful scientific experimentation, as opposed to detailed study of often inaccurate classical authors, has brought rich rewards. John Hunter, the anatomist, proved that it was physiologically impossible for a bird with lungs and air sacs designed to cope with atmospheric gases to survive under water for longer than a few minutes. The final nail in the coffin of the hibernating theory came with bird ringing, starting early in the twentieth century, initiated by the Danish ornithologist H. C. C. Mortensen. The results obtained by ringing swallows are instructive and interesting. The birds are either ringed as nestlings or trapped in delicate mist nets for the purpose.

Large numbers have to be ringed, for in the case of the swallow only 0.9 per cent of the rings are returned. Some ornithologists (not many) oppose ringing on the grounds that the ring may actually inconvenience the bird; ringers retaliate by saying that the rings are made of a very light alloy which does no damage. In fact bird ringing does occasionally result in the death of a bird; every ringer knows this — they will all remember occasional birds hanging dying in their mist nets, or actually dying in the hand whilst being ringed. But this is not to say that most of us are against ringing, because the knowledge it has brought us has resulted in ornithologists being able to give far more informed help in conserving birds which are under threat.

Next time you enjoy the view of swallows skimming over water or green meadow, remember that far back when all the land was covered by trees, *Hirundo rustica* was a rare bird searching for a cliff ledge on which to site its nest. When the doom-and-despondency brigade tell you man has ruined all the environment, just smile to yourself — and raise your hat to the next swallow you see!

5
Fresh Water

All living organisms, ourselves included, are made up of at least 70 per cent water which, with its delicate balance of dissolved elements, is the very stuff of life. In recent times we have greatly altered the quality of free water at the disposal of the flora and fauna; it has been a complex assault, creating more water here, removing some there, often abusing what has been there for centuries. We have drained the fens to make new farmlands and flooded prime farmland to make new reservoirs. Farm ponds have been filled in and have been disappearing at a great rate with the decline of mixed farming, and general streamlining of the industry. Ponds in fields were important breeding sites for amphibians, and their loss, along with wetland drainage, has been much to the detriment of frogs, toads and newts. In East Anglia, for instance, declines of up to 99 per cent have occurred in the frog population since the 1940s when the dig-for-victory campaign encouraged widespread reclamation of wetlands; the massive shift to cereals in later years intensified the same trend.

Three factors that have emerged in recent years have restored some hope for the amphibians. After the 1976 drought many farmers with livestock dug out new ponds in damp hollows as a precaution against water shortage. Secondly, the popularity of providing garden ponds has benefited amphibians of all kinds, especially the frog. Thirdly, gravel pits have been allowed to flood to make the devastation of the landscape more pleasing to the eye.

Life in our waters still faces great problems. Ditches, ponds and rivers have often become sumps for insecticides, fertilisers, silage and industrial effluents, variously impoverishing some and over-enriching others so that they choke up with water weeds and algae. Add to this all the leisure activities in which we now like to indulge in, on, or near water, and it adds up to a huge burden of adjustment for wildlife.

So we should look at how it has adapted, the losers and the winners. The study of freshwater ecology has grown apace with many of the problems, has helped intelligent campaigning against some of the

141

Borrowdale, Cumbria

worst excesses and leaves us better organised to monitor others.

Aquatic wildlife today needs to be seen in its various environments: rivers, lakes and reservoirs, and specially created environments which go some way to restoring the balance upset by man's activities in the other two. Estuary life is considered in Chapter 7 and canal life belongs to the urban environment (Chapter 8).

Rivers and River Management

River management is a term certain to raise the blood pressure of naturalists. The Countryside Act (Section II) and the Water Resources Act (Section 93) are both useful pieces of legislation to prevent pollution of large rivers, but they do not go far enough, since small rivers and streams are given insufficient protection. It is no good having stringent anti-pollution laws for large rivers if the tributaries that feed them are already polluted. A study I myself made of the effect of 'management' on a small river brought home what a lot we have to learn. Within a week of the commencement of operations the

The Ribble at Dunsop Bridge, Lancashire

lovely area had been dredged, trees which had dared to drop leaves into the pure water and thus increase its acidity were cut down and their roots grubbed out, 'Untidy'-looking meanders were straightened. Standing at one end I could see the water spread like a liquid ruler before me. But — it certainly was clean! Gone were the pools so beloved by the ever-watchful heron. Gone was the careless branch of willow on which perched the colourful kingfisher. Gone were the trickling shallows favoured by the wagtails and the white-bibbed dipper in search of stonefly and mayfly larvae. Gone were the sloping banks so suitable for the nesting sand martins. Gone were the pollarded willows and purple-budded alders so often full of titmice and wintering siskins. Gone was the marginal vegetation so useful to winter snipe and summer sandpipers. Gone was life.

The British Trust for Ornithology have realised the need to protect small streams and members have prepared a comprehensive list of some of particular value from the natural history point of view, although obviously biased towards birds. This list could be invaluable in the future as the demand for more and more water gains even greater momentum.

A naturalist taking a careful view of a river may think of it in four zones, starting from the source and working down.

Pied wagtail, common along riverbanks, as is its cousin the grey wagtail

The Headstream or Highland Brook

This is often an insignificant-looking zone as water oozes from the bowels of the earth ice-cold, often acidic and lacking in oxygen. In the main this remote habitat is of limited value to wildlife.

The Trout Beck

In this next zone torrential conditions are typical, as the water rushes downhill, often over solid rock. The trout is the only resident fish of the open water, and it often has to swim hard against the current merely to maintain its position. It is in this section that men sometimes build dams to produce hydro-electric power. These can be a great impediment to salmon migrating upstream to breed, but in some places, such as Pitlochry, ingenious bypasses called 'ladders' are constructed allowing the fish to make their way freely up and down stream. The miller's thumb, too, can be found sheltering behind stones here. These fish demand high oxygen concentration in the water, as does one of their

Green sandpiper

key prey species, the stonefly larva, which is one of the zone's most characteristic inhabitants. The dipper is the only bird capable of finding food, again often stonefly larvae, under bubbling gurgling water; it submerges by holding its wings at an angle to the current, thus being forced down. When it is ready to surface it simply pulls in its wings close to its body, and its natural buoyancy lifts it cork-like from the river bed. Given the speed of the current here, there is little if any rooted vegetation, although freshwater algae can gain a hold on the stones.

The Minnow Reach
The current is still fairly rapid here, and patches of silt or mud collect only around bends, where the slower flow does not sweep them away. A few species of flowering plant can live here, notably the water crowfoot. This is perhaps better named the river crowfoot since there

145

Bird under threat — the dipper

are some thirteen species of water crowfoot in Britain, nearly all with white flowers similar in shape to those of their close relative, the buttercup. Most of the crowfoots have two different types of leaf: large leaves which lie along the water surface and are responsible for photosynthesis, and long submerged leaves which drag like anchor chains, enabling the plant to maintain its position even in a strong current.

The Lowland Reach

This is the slow, meandering region, and except following periods of excessive rainfall, all is peaceful here. But man's activities are most threatening in this area — both industrial and sporting enterprises. The sewage from most towns ends up in rivers, as does industrial effluent, so that many, particularly in England, have become so filthy that life has ceased to exist in them; indeed some are a positive health hazard to those unfortunate enough to live close to the banks.

The pollution comes from three main sources. Firstly, raw sewage

Trout Beck, Ribblesdale

Dipper

discharged into water begins to decay as a result of bacterial action. This process uses up oxygen, and in areas of high sewage outfall there will be insufficient oxygen left even for invertebrates, and all living organisms will choke in the river of excrement. The cure for this is simple but expensive — constructing more treatment works to deal with the sewage prior to its reaching the river. Many local authorities say the cost is too high. To this we must reply, 'How expensive is life itself?' As a student of biology in London during the late 1950s, I remember strolling along the banks of the Thames feeling sick with the stench which crept out of the river as a choking smog. On days of high wind, white suds of detergent foam drifted about and added its stinking load to the sordid scene. This positive menace was not allowed to continue: two of Europe's biggest and most up-to-date sewage-treatment works were constructed three miles below Woolwich, one on either side of the filthy river. The effect of building

148

Water crowfoot

Beckton and Cross Ness has been truly dramatic. By 1963 huge flocks of teal, pochard and even shelduck were found as high up the river as Tower Bridge. Their presence was a sure sign that the invertebrate fauna had returned, since birds will not stay where there is no food. The food chains were restored. Swans sailed upriver and the population around Greenwich now often exceeds 500. In 1968 large numbers of terns were recorded at West Thurrock, and in the same year the first smelt since 1910 was noted at Fulham and a bass was caught at Blackwall Point. West Thurrock was again in the news in 1974 as the first salmon for 100 years was captured, and in 1976 a seahorse was found at Dagenham, a first for the Thames! The success story has continued and has been well documented. If this progress was possible in the Thames then it is surely possible in all our rivers.

The second source of pollution is from chemical effluents drained into the rivers from industry. These may be poisonous in their own

Lowland reach — Brierfield near Nelson, Lancashire

right, as for example the drainage from factories producing acids, alkalis or heavy metals, or they may be more subtle. Two factories may each produce a chemical which on its own is harmless, but when these mix in the river the resulting reaction between them may produce a lethal product, and one much harder to detect.

Thirdly there is the problem of thermal pollution, particularly evident around areas such as power stations. Water is extracted from a river, used to cool the generators and then channelled back into the river. This water can raise the temperature to a level which is lethal to most forms of wildlife (although a moderate increase, together with the upwelling, may create conditions positively beneficial to aquatic life). Excessive thermal pollution can lower oxygen levels in the water and produce a barrier through which fish and invertebrates cannot pass, preventing the movement of fish such as salmon and trout to their breeding grounds. The provision of cooling towers, although they are often unsightly, can lower the water temperature sufficiently to prevent this thermal barrier from developing.

Once the river is cool, clear, and relatively unpolluted, the only problem facing wildlife is the competition with man's own leisure activities. Compromise is again the answer. There should be room for the skilled and affluent angler, the not-so-skilled or not-so-affluent, and the kid with the bent pin. There must be room for the birds to sing and

Trough of Bowland, Lancashire

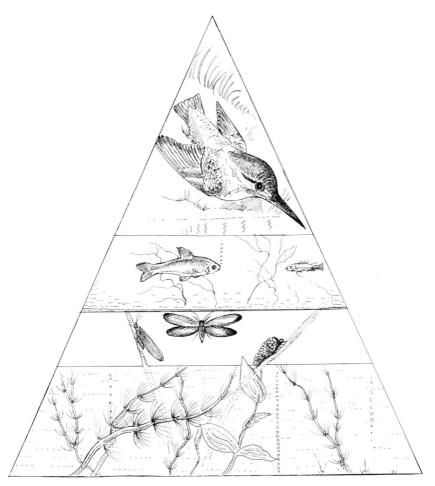

Food pyramid for fresh water; with kingfisher, fish, caddis fly and water weeds

the otter to whistle his love call to the winter's moon. We must make room and we must make time to stand and stare at one of our greatest natural assets — the lovely rolling riversides of Britain. Wordsworth would now recognise the view of the water, if not the surroundings, from his Westminster Bridge, but would the old brigade recognise the Irwell and the Trent, the Mersey and the Tyne, the Calder and the Humber?

The state of our rivers can often be judged from the population of wildlife which they support. The actual detection of pollution by appearance is no easy matter since highly dangerous water can often *look* perfectly clean. It is here that the naturalist can prove of great assistance. Pollution will affect the organisms living in the water and

A young angler trying his luck near Flatford Mill

153

Mute swan incubating

cause their populations to decline. With small species, often difficult to identify, a quantitative estimate is difficult to obtain. For pollution indicators, therefore, what are needed are populations of large, more-or-less-resident, easy-to-count species. What better for this than birds? Two useful species here are the mute swan (*Cygnus olor*) and the kingfisher (*Alcedo atthis*). The former is a vegetarian and will only occur where there is ample water weed, and the kingfisher's continued presence denotes an adequate fish population and a healthy system of food chains. (The numbers of these birds will obviously also be affected by human population density, and so the results are not on their own the whole answer).

The magnificent swan has an 8 foot wingspan, the longest of any British bird. To hear swans flying overhead, kept in contact with each other by the sound of air surging through their primary feathers is an ever-delightful experience.

Swans were originally kept in a semi-feral state (especially by the Crown) for their food value, but today they are a wild species in many places, less protected from the pressures on our multi-purpose waterways. If we look at their way of life, we see what kinds of protection they, and many other birds, need.

Cygnet and parent

Swans become territory-conscious in February and by April their nest site has been established. The nesting material is not brought any great distance but vegetation within reach, such as water weeds and reeds, is pulled together into a heap. The male or cob (the bigger bird and with a larger knob at the base of his bill) initiates the building, the female — or pen — completes it, keeping the nest high to avoid flooding. A failed site is abandoned but a successful one is kept for many years, one site on record being occupied by the same pair for 14 years. Breeding begins at the age of three. After a display period, the female is held beneath the water during copulation which occurs more often than would be necessary merely to fertilise the eggs, the process serving to strengthen the pair bond. It takes seven months for the family to be raised, and as many as 40 per cent of swans' nests are thought to be predated by children — despite the obvious dangers of drowning and the attacks of angry birds.

The territorial behaviour of the birds seems to be based on food availability following hatching, since at Abbotsbury in Dorset, where swans live in 'managed' conditions and eel grass is present in vast quantities, the birds actually nest colonially and defend much smaller areas.

The swan population was up to 1955 showing a 16 per cent annual

increase, but has declined since then; the population is now somewhere around 15,000. This drop is possibly due to pollution of lakes and rivers, but more probably due to the pressures on the species of human activities. Breeding success may well be hindered by disturbance from holidaymakers. The incubation, mainly carried out by the female, lasts for thirty-five days, the eggs being turned regularly and occasionally splashed with weed to maintain a satisfactory humidity. A day after hatching the young are led to the water. The mute swan at this stage is far from mute, as the cygnets learn to recognise their parents' voices; the young themselves have a number of different sounds, to signify contentment, fear, hunger and so on. They are born with an insurance policy of about five days' supply of fat in their bodies, and an instinct to search for and peck at food, an urge which must be developed sufficiently if they are to survive these critical early days. There is a high mortality rate between the sixth and the tenth day following hatching. The parents may help a little by chopping grass for their young, but this is not a regular habit and does not last for long. Though in the early stages the parents allow the young to ride on their backs, some are still taken by pike, and some in coastal areas by the greater black-backed gull.

Ice can be another hazard for cygnets in cold seasons. They cannot walk on it, but try for long periods to swim through it and merely gyrate. Unless they adjust, they will not survive. In really cold weather, mass migration to the coast takes place, as salt-marsh plants and seaweeds are almost always available there. When about seven months old, the cygnets are driven off by the cob who is becoming territory-conscious once more and now feels threatened by his offspring. The juveniles then disperse and gather in adolescent flocks. At two years old they start the process of finding a mate, and breed at three. But only two out of each twenty hatched birds reach maturity and it is a lucky bird that reaches twenty years of age.

Pylons are one of the constant hazards to mature swans. They fly into the wires and over 50 per cent of adult deaths are due to this cause. Another increasingly frequent threat to the mute swan and other wildfowl is the vast amount of discarded fishing tackle left lying about. The lead weights cause many deaths by poisoning the blood stream, whilst hooks and nylon line may entangle the bill and prevent feeding. The cygnets are particularly vulnerable while they learn what is edible and what is not. The problem is aggravated by the fact that discarded fishing line is non-biodegradable and remains a potential danger for many, many years. In some popular fishing areas, at Trent Bridge, Nottingham, for example, no mute swans at all are in evidence

Fishing line removed from a cygnet's bill and throat: 5 metres (16ft) of line, three hooks and 8 lethal lead weights

Kingfisher

where once they were common. Another problem the swans have had to contend with is the constant traffic of pleasure boats on so many of our navigable rivers, creating great disturbance, and eroding the banks into steep escarpments which impede the escape, or even leisurely exit, of the birds from the water.

A more colourful, and in some ways even more vulnerable, species is the kingfisher, 'the great splendour of the brooks' as Tennyson called it, with its iridescent blue-green back and orange front. The kingfisher family consists of over 80 species but only one breeds in Britain — and this one is now facing problems, especially in polluted areas of the northern counties. Clean rivers, the haunts of so many creatures such as the water vole, the heron, the pied and grey wagtails, also abound with bullheads and minnows, the favourite prey of the kingfisher. This 5½ inch (13cm) bundle of colour is a deadly killer of fish. It dives from a vantage point — is successful 33 per cent of the times — brings up a fish in its long daggerlike bill, bangs it on the head and swallows it

Swans soon take advantage of even busy rivers, providing pollution is kept in check

head-first. This prevents gill covers or other spiny protuberances from blocking the gullet. The indigestible parts are coughed back in the form of a pellet.

Its breeding period begins fairly late. Once it has selected a site, usually on a sheer bank of a river containing good stocks of food material, the tunnel is excavated by both sexes; they hurl themselves at the bank until a satisfactory foothold has been produced. Their feet have two toes fused together, ideal for shovelling — and no doubt for swimming under water. The 2 foot (60 centimetre) tunnel, with nesting chamber at the end, takes five or six days to excavate. On the eighth day following the commencement of tunnel-building, the pair mate, as they do on subsequent days up to the laying of the final egg of the clutch (about six). Copulation is preceded by the cock feeding the hen with a fish, which he presents to her head-first: this used to be thought of as purely a symbolic act, strengthening the pair bond, but it is probably highly functional, building up the female's body reserves for the eggs she must make, and lay, one a day. The young hatch in about fifteen days, then receive about six whole fish per day, some being almost as large as the young themselves. This keeps both parents very busy: they take mainly minnow, stickleback and bullheads but they will not refuse trout fry, thereby attracting persecution by anglers and fish farmers. For the kingfisher, however, this is a minor problem compared to pollution. Oily effluents kill caddis fly, a favoured diet of the bullhead and minnow, which, in turn reduces the food of the kingfisher: the tissue of the web of life is eroded away. Sewage causes reduction in oxygen levels (impoverishing the fauna), detergents cause problems by breaking down the surface tension of the water on which many insects depend, and again the kingfisher, at the vulnerable end of the food chain, bears the brunt.

At three weeks the young are ready to emerge from the nest tunnel and are recognisable as kingfishers — not so gaudy as their parents, but bright none the less. Their bills are shorter than those of the adult and their fishing is inexpert, with a success rate of merely 5 per cent. As the days pass, their skill of course improves rapidly, but not all make the transition to independence — some actually drown or become so waterlogged they freeze to death at night. Add to this the presence of stoat, weasel, sparrowhawk and tawny owl, and you can see that the first weeks of life must be hazardous even if man does not make things worse.

In 1963 the kingfisher was reduced almost to extinction by the severe winter which iced over its foraging grounds. But in the next four years its numbers recovered, due almost certainly to the greater availability of food to a small population. In the north of England this recovery was slower due to greater pollution problems.

Lakes and Reservoirs

Natural lakes have been coveted for many years by the developing, ever-thirsty conurbations of the large cities: for instance, Thirlmere and Windermere in the Lake District. Some southern cities still rely very much on abstraction from rivers, but others, along with their northern counterparts, look to upland sources. When these are not available reservoirs need to be constructed. The wild creatures dependent upon lakes, natural or artificial, have slightly different requirements.

All forms of life on earth require water for their own biological processes; only one, man the tool-maker, also needs water for industry, domestic use and leisure. There will be periods of little if any demand alternating with periods of insatiable 'thirst'. Thus water must be stored. To the water planners, the surface area of a water store is not the important factor: it is the volume which is crucial, and the vital factor is therefore depth. Wild things, on the other hand, require shallow water where adequate vegetation can root and its dependent invertebrates occur. Thus we have a potential source of conflict between the water resources boards and the conservationists whenever a new storage area is being considered. Firstly the argument revolves around the initial flooding of an ecologically important valley; then, once it has been decided to flood, the debate hinges around the acceptable depth of the flooding.

It has been calculated that by the year 2000 Britain's demand for water will be close to 60 million cubic metres per day. If power stations were built near the coast and salt water used for cooling, demand could be reduced: I can hardly wait for the outcry to begin if this is tried at Frinton, Brighton or Blackpool! It is no good doing an ostrich act, however, burying our heads in the coastal sand, for industry's water has to come from somewhere, and wherever that is it will affect us or our wildlife.

The annual rainfall over the whole country averages out at about 35 inches (90cm). After evaporation and transpiration from the leaves of plants, the residual water level is around 15mm, which would make about 200 million cubic metres available per day — far more than the forecast demand by the year 2000. But the rainfall is not evenly spread over the country or over the twelve months of the year. Again, therefore, the problem is one of distribution and storage, rather than supply. Barrages are at times considered: Solway, Morecambe Bay, Dee and Wash were subjected to feasibility studies and a greedy eye was cast in the direction of my own home estuary, the Duddon. But estuarine-barrage schemes, conservation objections apart, present great problems, including the expense of construction and prevention

Morecambe Bay — threatened by a barrage

of pollution. So for the moment the most economic method of storing water still seems to be by constructing more reservoirs and increasing the capacity of those we already have. Large stretches of water are always eagerly accepted by wildlife. Birds such as gulls and pochards roost in the middle and feed at the edges, if vegetation is allowed to grow there, or dive for fish in deeper water, as do goosanders, goldeneyes and grebes. Man also finds the habitat irresistible, and anglers, shooters and birdwatchers compete for access. The problems posed by such multiple demands on reservoirs and some possible solutions can be seen at the Brent Reservoir in North London, and the Grafham Water, 50 miles due north of London. Both these stretches are faced with great human pressure, as are all lakes and large stretches of water close to our cities. The growth of the motorway systems have made them even more vulnerable.

Brent Reservoir
Leo Batten has made a special study of Brent, in particular considering the conflict between birds and yachts. Many questions must be answered, but the main one is what percentage of the total water can be sailed upon without disturbing the birds? Some species will be affected more than others — which ones?

The Brent Reservoir, sometimes called the Jew's Harp, was

162

Tufted duck at Brent

constructed between 1833 and 1837. It belongs to the British Waterways Board and has been sailed upon since 1888. The number of boats based at Brent has increased to 300, though 50 is the maximum number allowed on the water at any one time. Until 1963 only a small area was given over to sailing, but then this was extended, leaving only the shallow eastern end for the birds. No part of the reservoir is screened from yachts. The disturbance is felt by some species more than others. The great crested grebe, for example, has not bred on Brent since 1963, though before this date there were always two and perhaps three pairs. The annual regatta held on the Brent is the only occasion when a motor boat is allowed on the water — but the regatta occurs right at the height of the breeding season and many birds then desert. Little grebes, surprisingly, are less disturbed, breeding annually; one winter flock reached over 130. Gulls, mainly black-headed, tend to use the reservoir as a night roost but late boaters disturb them and send them off to other reservoirs where boating is not allowed. Should these other reservoirs yield to people's increasing demands for boating space, it is conceivable that the flight lines of the gulls might be directed towards the airport, with the great danger of bird strikes causing accidents. The water rails and moorhens preferring the shallow, marshy end are not affected. The coots are disturbed but are quite tolerant and allow boats to pass fairly near. The smew are also tolerant, but pochard and especially tufted ducks are soon put to flight.

Grafham Water
This is a manmade area, constructed in the early 1960s by damming a valley; the water comes from the Great Ouse. It is about 2½ miles (4km) long by 1 mile (1.5km) wide, has 10 miles (16km) of shoreline and a surface area of 628 hectares. A reserve area, comprising 2–3 per cent of the water surface, is set aside for birds, including a series of fairly shallow creeks. Studies have been going on for some years to find the areas preferred by each species.

Most of Grafham is over 30ft (10 metres) deep, and it is exposed and wave-battered in the middle, so that the birds tend to gather in the creeks. It is so large that disturbed birds do not leave the water, as they do at other lakes, but merely move along. The two main sources of disturbance at Grafham are sailing and fishing, the sailing season extending from April until October and fishing, for the very sizeable trout with which the water was deliberately stocked, taking place during the same months. A number of fishing boats are available for hire.

The boats are not allowed to enter the creeks, which may help birdwatchers by concentrating the flocks. The fishing season may assist this trend further, since the anglers are excluded from the reserve area. At this stage ornithologists can be detrimental to the birds, as careless and noisy stalking will flush the birds from their refuges. The effect of weekend pressure can be seen by the following wildfowl counts:

> Thursday — about 300
> Sunday — about 90
> Tuesday — about 450

Beyond Grafham is a series of sludge lagoons, which are good for nesting waders. The public used to insist on picnicking on the grassy islands, despite the dangers of walking along a thin crust concealing two metres of 'quicksand' to reach them. The area thus had to be fenced off, and this had a dramatic effect on breeding birds. The little ringed plover, for example, went from 6 breeding pairs to 17, and the redshank population doubled from 6 to 12 pairs.

Great crested grebe

The Great Crested Grebe

Anyone interested in reading about Grafham should consult Dr Arnold Cooke's splendid booklet *The Birds of Grafham Water* (see Bibliography). Here again it is reported that the great crested grebe often attempts to breed, but without success. Can we not help this nervous species?

The grebes are a fascinating order of birds which ornithologists call Podicipediformes. From an evolutionary point of view it is a very ancient order. The birds' wings are short, so that they are not efficient fliers, whilst on land they have difficulty in walking, since the legs are set so far back on the body. Indeed this is the origin of the name Podicipediformes. The tibia is actually held within the body muscle, rather than being free to move, as in other birds. Thus freedom of movement on land has been sacrificed to enable supreme efficiency of aquatic motion, especially the underwater pursuit of prey. Even the tail feathers are much reduced.

If ever the fortunes of a species have been determined by its feathers, then that species must surely be the great crested grebe. Its feathers wear very rapidly and the plumage soon resembles the fur of a mammal. In times gone by grebe pelts were used in the manufacture of

165

Wigeon

muffs and as linings for overcoats — known as 'grebe fur'. The function of these 'furry' feathers is obviously to provide the efficient insulation so essential to an aquatic species. In breeding plumage, the grebe has a most delightful head pattern consisting of chestnut-coloured ear tufts and a frill round the neck rather similar to an Elizabethan ruff. These were much favoured in the nineteenth century when thousands of birds were killed; often the whole body of the bird was mounted on top of ladies' hats for festive occasions. In the wild, the grebe displays its tuft to spectacular advantage in the dramatic courtship dance, one of the most elaborate rituals of any British bird.

Another peculiarity of the great crested grebe long known to ornithologists was noted in 1911 by W. P. Pyecraft:

One peculiarity the great crested grebe shares with the congeners and this is the use of feathers instead of grit or stones for digestive purposes—that is to say, in the comminution of its food. I have never dissected a grebe whose stomach did not contain feathers, always those of the breast. Why they should display this singular habit is beyond hope of discovery and is not the less puzzling because no other birds, other than the Grebe tribe, are known to adopt this strange habit of feather eating, save in the case of captive birds wherein it represents a disorganised condition of health, as

166

in the case of parrots, for example. It would seem that the feathers are not disgorged in the shape of pellets as in the case of owls and hawks which swallow a certain percentage of the feathers of their victims, but that they are slowly digested. But whereas the bolus thrown up by the raptorial birds has formed in the crop, that which is so commonly met with in the grebes is always found in the stomach, whence rejection is impossible. I have never taken stones or grit from the gizzards of grebes.

In 1980 our knowledge has not increased very much. We know that feather eating is not an accidental result of preening, because feathers are fed to young birds from the second day following hatching. The habit is thought to aid digestion in some way, and may help to protect the gut from sharp bones of the fish which form such an important proportion of the grebe's diet.

In 1850 the population of the great crested grebe was becoming desperately depleted; in 1860 it was thought to be down to about 32 pairs. But it did benefit somewhat from three Acts passed to protect birds between 1870 and 1880. Full protection was given in 1880 and by 1931 the number had risen to just over 1,100 pairs. We now have over 2,000 pairs and despite pollution and disturbance the future for this species looks bright. Man, for once, has learned that all the grebe needs is fairly shallow water, and some peace and quiet to carry out the complex breeding ritual. We are even learning to create habitat from areas we no longer need, not least from disused gravel pits.

Specially Created Habitats

In 1956 Dr Jeffrey Harrison, who until his untimely death in 1979 was an ardent wildfowler, but also a conservationist, initiated a scheme at a gravel pit near Sevenoaks in Kent which has had far-reaching effects. He learned how to create suitable habitats for wildfowl, which must of course benefit other wildlife. The area of water was extended and tree cover planted to screen factories. Blackberries planted at the water's edge suited mallards, which are very partial to the fruit, and no doubt the prickles deterred fishermen from moving into sheltered areas. 'Loafing spots' were provided so that birds could leave the water at will, especially when it was rough. Artificial islands were made and anchored in the deep stretches; nesting rafts have attracted grebes, mallard, tufted ducks, Canada geese and greylags, and have the added advantage of being out of range of fishermen and mammalian predators such as stoats and foxes. The botanical community at the refuge deserves special mention. The wildfowlers had their shot birds examined and the seed in their crops identified, so a 'menu' of favourable plants could be drawn up. Dabbling ducks like teal and wigeon relish reed grass, mare's tail, giant water dock and amphibious bistort. Stonewort is a favourite of diving ducks such as pochard, while tufted duck and goldeneye benefit from the invertebrate life encouraged by any underwater plants. The outlook for their offspring can also be improved quite simply by providing many of these same plants, for they swarm with palatable insects in the summer months. Duckweed literally makes excellent duckling fodder. A growth of pond sedge provides good cover from marauding crows and other aerial predators, and at the same time prevents pike from reaching the shallows. By attending to all these details, the duck population, and no doubt that of other animals, has been increased five-fold. The discovery of alder and silver birch seeds in some ducks' crops led to these tree species being planted by the water's edge — and to the appearance of siskins and redpolls to feed on them too. Redpolls and bearded tits are also attracted to willowherb left to flourish near the margin.

The overall physical structure of the gravel pit has been altered. Male mallards claim their territories on water, not on land, and it was found that two pairs can nest side by side just so long as one male cannot see the other from his water station. Knowing this, a bit of landscaping can maximise mallard density: a gravel pit with many bays allows a higher population to co-exist happily than a circular one where every male can see all his neighbours. Further landscaping, with shingle banks, and open rides amongst the trees, suits waders — sandpipers, dunlin, redshank and woodcock are easily encouraged. Some compromises can be worked out between our demand for water and that of wildlife.

6

Mountains and Moorlands

Our splendid high lands receive far more rain and snow than more sheltered parts; they serve both as sources of rivers and as catchment areas for lakes and reservoirs. These upland zones often have a delicate ecological balance (which we disrupt at our peril). The soils are almost always shallow, acid and lacking in nutrients, especially lime. This accounts for many attributes of the vegetation — particularly the insectivorous habit of sundew and butterwort. In winter the ground is frozen hard, and the summers are so short that colonisation is slow to start and difficult to maintain. Once disturbed it may take years for plants to recover. A few years ago great concern was expressed when some of the Alaskan perma-frost ground was disturbed by warm oil pipelines; on a lesser scale, but still of great importance, is the damage done by ski-runs, already evident on the Scottish Cairngorms. Here some efforts have been made to help eroded vegetation to creep back by spraying the ground with appropriate grass seeds in a binding solution of bitumen. These upland areas, so easily damaged, should be conserved — for water catchment, sporting and walking interests, forestry and last but not least their often unique wildlife. If carefully managed these need not always be in conflict.

With water catchment in mind, large areas of sphagnum bog should be maintained. Secondly, the high lands are an important resource supporting red grouse, red deer and sheep in large numbers. In Chapter 4 I mentioned the possibility of using rabbits as a food crop for export, and the same approach could be used to control the numbers of red deer, now increasing so quickly as to cause concern to the forester who is busily planting many of our upland areas — a practice discussed in Chapter 1.

We now have more leisure time and our hilltops are beckoning more and more people. Whatever route they choose, there is obviously a funnelling effect as they tramp up to the summit, and it is just here that many of the rare life forms occur.

Walkers, often oblivious to the wildlife of the area, can cause mild

Pendleside near Clitheroe

disturbance or total catastrophe. Slow-growing plant life which may have taken years to establish a precarious existence can be trampled underfoot; once demolished, the vulnerable skin of tundra vegetation is virtually unable to recover, rain and high winds quickly eroding whatever soil is there. The food chain has been broken at the first link. Rare breeding birds such as the golden eagle, merlin, greenshank, peregrine, snow bunting and dotterel may be disturbed to such an extent that they do not successfully incubate their eggs. The effect upon the mammals may not be so obvious, but the shy, delightful mountain hare is often the first to be adversely affected.

Due to their ability to survive in what to us, at least, seems a hostile environment, the plants and animals found at high altitude hold a special fascination for naturalists. A careful look at just a few of them will show just how precarious their existence is and will underline the importance of maintaining areas where they can continue to prosper undisturbed.

Few British trees are able to survive high up the hills, but one

Langdale, Cumbria

Food pyramid for mountain and moorland areas; with heather, mountain hare and golden eagle

notable exception is the rowan; and a few stunted birches or ash trees may hold on. The majority of upland areas, however, are dominated by grasses, particularly sheep's fescue, mat grass and the bents. The very damp areas will be covered by sedges such as cotton grass and bog moss, drier tracts of moorland by heather or purple moor grass. Flowering plants have to be tough to thrive here, but two species are able to cope and are well worth careful study. These are the bog asphodel and the butterwort.

The plants, especially heather, are but the first link in the food chain,

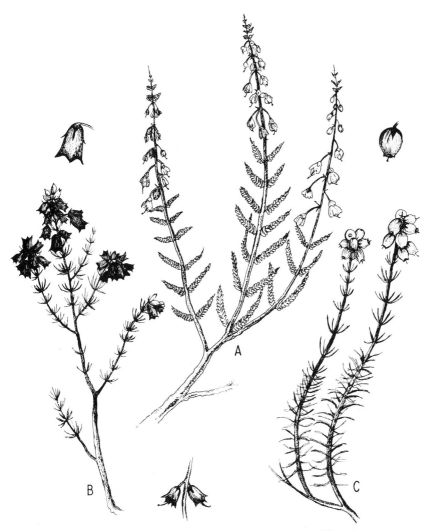

A heather or ling, B bell heather, C cross-leaved heath

being fed upon by many interesting insects including the brown argus, the large heath butterfly and the attractive emperor moth. Also feeding upon the heather are the mountain hare, red grouse and ptarmigan, whilst soaring overhead we may be lucky enough to see birds of prey — even merlin, hen harrier and golden eagle.

The part played by heather in the ecology of these regions is important. Heather is a name used loosely for several separate species. Cross-leaved heath (*Erica tetralix*) is found in boggy areas, and on the drier ground below 2,200 feet (600 metres) are patches of bell heather

(*Erica cinerea*); the pale purple common heather (*Calluna vulgaris*) is the one which dominates Britain's grouse moors and is the matrix that protects and feeds the rest of the upland community and upon which the shooting industry is based. It is not only man's industry which thrives on these heathered heights. *Calluna vulgaris*, also called ling, flowers in July and August, humming with nectar-seeking bees. The air is throbbing with the golden-winged dragonfly or, as darkness descends on the hills, with the high-pitched notes of hordes of hungry midges which can make these upland regions so unpleasant to the warm-blooded mammals on whom the female insects feed.

Appreciation of how some wildlife can survive on mountains and moorlands, despite the difficulties of climate and soil, can be gleaned from a close study of a few species.

Upland Plants

The scientific name for the rowan or mountain ash is *Sorbus aucuparia*. Sorbus means apple and the tree cannot also be an ash; in fact mountain ash is not an appropriate name but it is easy to see how it came about. The leaves of the rowan are more delicate than those of the ash but the two are remarkably similar in shape. Each leaf consists of between nine and fifteen leaflets, one standing alone at the tip and the rest arranged in opposite pairs. The fruits, however, are completely different from those of the ash, rowan developing tiny red 'apples' which are the special favourites of the migrant birds arriving in the autumn. The birds swallow the fruit whole, digest the flesh and, perhaps after they have travelled some miles, pass out the seeds in their droppings, thus acting as important agents of dispersal, and certainly the only way of spreading the tree's progeny uphill. The dry fruits of the ash, on the other hand, are carried by the wind.

Rowan never grows very tall, exceptionally reaching about 50 feet (up to about 15 metres). When caught by angled sunlight the smooth grey bark shines and flashes like metal. The creamy-white blossom is made up of separate flowers, each bearing five white petals. The scent is described by many as unpleasant; however it serves its purpose, attracting the insects which pollinate the flowers.

Throughout Europe the rowan has been associated with magic and superstition for centuries, and in Britain we have a large number of vernacular names including shepherd's friend, whistle wood (whistles were made from the hollowed bark), witch hazel and quick-beam. In Yorkshire, Wales and Ireland rowans were planted in churchyards to prevent the dead from rising. Also in Yorkshire, 2 May was celebrated as 'Rowan Tree Witch Day', when houses were hung with branches and milk was stirred with a twig of rowan to prevent the evil ones from

174

Rowan: blossom (above) and fruit (below)

curdling it. The tree is not only held in veneration by man, but is of great use to the wild things, as a fourteenth-century Irish poem indicates:

> Glen of the rowan trees with scarlet berries,
> With fruit sought by every flock of birds,
> A sleeping paradise for every badger,
> Silent in their quiet sets with their young.

The bog asphodel (*Narthecium ossifragum*) is a member of the lily family, found in bogs and acid soils in the north and west. At one time it had the name *Asphodelus lancastriae*, probably because in the

175

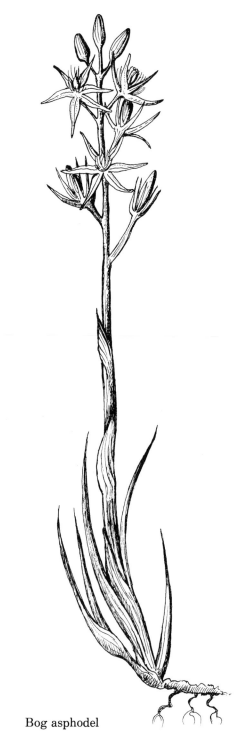

Bog asphodel

Butterwort

seventeenth century Lancashire lasses gathered it from the moors to make a dye for their hair. This is where its vernacular names of maidenhair and yellow grass originate. The name *ossifragum*, bone-breaking, is also of interest: bog asphodel was thought to soften the bones of the cattle which ate it.

Despite its evil reputation this attractive plant, its star-shaped flower composed of petals yellow above and a delicate green below, often adds the only spark of colour to the green of a high damp moorland. A perennial, it may be found in bloom from July to September, and often when the flowers have faded they are replaced by rich orange seed pods.

Also a perennial, the butterwort (*Pinguicula vulgaris*) tends to flower in similar habitats, but earlier than the bog asphodel, usually from May to July. The old herbalist Gerard has plenty to tell us about its

177

properties: 'The husband-mens' wives of Yorkshire do use to anoint the dugs (udders) of their kine with the fat of oilus juice of the herbe butterwort, when they are bitten with any venemous worm, or chapped, rifted or hurt by any other means.' In the North Country the leaves are steeped in milk to curdle and thicken it, a practice also employed by the Lapps. Well versed in the use of their native herbs, they pour cow or reindeer milk on to the leaves and leave it to coagulate for a day or two before eating the nourishing mess.

Growing on high bleak moorlands, with much of the goodness leached out of the soil by the high rainfall, the butterwort has difficulty in obtaining sufficient nitrogenous material to build up its body proteins. The way in which it has solved this problem is fascinating. The leaves, which grow from a rosette, secrete tiny droplets of an adhesive fluid. These trap insects, and as the creatures struggle to free themselves, the leaf is stimulated to curve inwards and create a temporary 'stomach'. Digestive juices are then produced and the plant absorbs all of the insect's body, full of valuable proteins, save for the hard chitinous exo-skeleton. Thus butterwort is an example of an insectivorous plant, making up for a nitrogen deficiency by trapping its own food. This is also done by sundew, another plant found on our wet mountains and moorlands.

Butterwort's scientific name *Pinguicula* derives from the Latin *pinquis*, fat. This obviously relates to the slippery feel of the foliage and may have given it the name buttery-wort. Personally, however, I feel it is derived from its use for converting milk to 'butter'.

An Upland Insect

These high moors may be lacking in numbers of species, but those plants which can live there are often plentiful, a fact which the insect life has not been slow to notice. Many moths therefore thrive at high altitudes, and the most attractive of these is the emperor moth (*Saturnia pavonia*). It is found on the wing from as early as April, the male being much more active and a lot smaller than the female. He tends also to be on the wing during the hours of daylight, flitting amongst the heather, but the female usually remains quiet until the evening. It is then that her pheromone of scent is carried on the heavy moorland air, often attracting as many as fifty suitors wishing to mate with her.

The eggs are laid around the stem of the larval food plant, usually heather. Until they are about three months old the larvae are gregarious, but soon after this they begin to shun the company of others. They are handsome creatures, basically green in colour, and so camouflaged from eager meadow pipits, skylarks and wheatears which

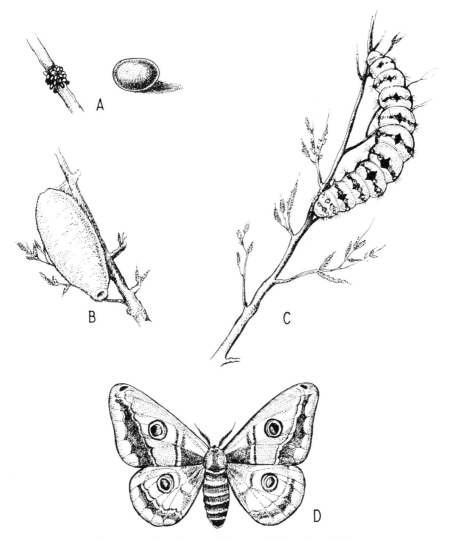

Emperor moth: A egg, B pupa, C larva, D adult

rear their families on our highlands. An emperor caterpillar has on each segment a pink tubercle ringed with black from which springs a cluster of short hairs.

The emperor is Britain's only silk moth, the flask-shaped pupal case being spun of brown silk which matches perfectly the stems of the background heather plants, again giving maximum cryptic protection to the developing moth. The pupae can remain inactive for almost two years, under snow or sun, before emerging as splendid adults to breed and all too soon to perish. Each wing, upper and lower, has a large eye-catching spot similar to those on a peacock's wing; and as the old word for a peacock was *pavonia* the scientific name for the species, and others in the same genus, makes sense. The other half of the name is more difficult to unravel but the goddess Juno, who loved peacocks, was sometimes called Saturnia.

Animals and Birds

To go into suspended animation is one way of combating adverse weather conditions and another is to migrate. Yet another is to wrap up warm and get on with living. This latter strategy has been adopted by the mountain hare and the ptarmigan, both of which feed on heather. They have, however, had to solve one very great problem — when snow covers their chosen habitat they are very easily seen. Both species, mammal and bird, have come up with the same solution — they too must become white.

Pliny records that the white fur of the mountain hare (*Lepus timidus*) in winter is caused by the animal eating snow — but that explanation will hardly suit us today! The brown hare and the mountain hare differ in both choice of habitat and physical appearance. The mountain hare is seldom seen at altitudes below 1,200 feet (400 metres) and in Britain was mainly restricted to the Highlands of Scotland, Ireland and the Isle of Man. In the 1880s it was introduced into some elevated areas in England and Wales. According to Yalden (1971) some of these colonies may now be struggling to survive, but I have watched a population in the Pennines above Saddleworth for some years and no decrease has been obvious.

The mountain hare is smaller and stockier than its lowland cousin, and there is no black top to the bob tail, which is so much a feature of the brown hare. Their pelage colour differs at all times of year. The winter white of *timidus* can easily appear as early as mid-October and persist until well into May, but in most individuals it lasts for a much shorter period. Its summer coat is grey-blue as opposed to the brown of *Lepus capensis*. The mountain hare found in Ireland is a distinct sub-species called *Lepus timidus hibernicus*; it has a decidedly rusty-looking coat and does not turn completely white in the winter.

The hares and rabbits are an interesting group to study. At one time they were included in the order Rodentia, but because they had a tiny second upper incisor which no other rodent possessed they were placed in their own sub-order, Duplicidentata. Other vital distinctions were soon discovered, including the fact that true rodents only have enamel on the front of their incisor teeth, whereas rabbits, hares and pikas have it at both back and front, and never develop the chisel-shaped gnawing teeth so typical of rodents. The teeth do, however, keep growing throughout life and continuous use is essential

Mountain hare

if they are not to grow towards and even into the opposite jaws, condemning the animal to a painful death. For those and other more complex reasons the hares and rabbits now constitute their own order, the Lagomorpha.

The main food of the mountain hare consists of heather shoots, and like the other lagomorphs it exhibits the phenomenon of refection. To a hygienically but not very scientifically minded person, the idea of an animal consuming its own faeces is often revolting, and I know of one perfumed lady who gave away all four of her children's pet rabbits when she discovered 'what they were up to'. In fact the animals have no option. The digestive system of lagomorphs is not capable of breaking down the tough cellulose plant cells in the time it takes for the material to pass through the gut. The pellets which emerge from the anus are wet and still full of essential food. Such pellets are usually produced during the day, are immediately eaten, allowing the partially digested material to be dealt with more effectively. The night droppings are usually dry, showing that the lagomorph has now extracted the maximum nutrients from the vegetation, often gathered from open and therefore potentially dangerous habitat, full of lurking foxes, stoats and birds of prey.

Lagomorphs, in common with many other mammals, possess one other fascinating feature, this time concerned with the reproductive cycle, which in the mountain hare can commence as early as December. After a gestation period of about fifty days, two or occasionally three young are born. Should a period of hard weather occur, however, the pregnancy is terminated, and the developing embryos are reabsorbed into the mother's bloodstream — even if the pregnancy is well advanced. This has a very important evolutionary advantage, preventing the young being brought into a world in which they would have no chance of survival. The doe must also benefit from the food material recovered in this way.

Even at birth the leverets have open eyes and are covered with fur; within ten days they can lead an independent existence. Newborn rabbits are much less advanced, but have the shelter of a burrow.

Like the mountain hare, but possibly in response to slightly different climatic factors, the ptarmigan (*Lagopus mutus*) — a close relation of the red grouse — moults three times during the year. The breeding plumage, assumed during March and April and complete by the end of May, is basically of a mottled brown, but the wings are white and are particularly obvious when the bird flies. At the end of July when the breeding season is over, a bluish-grey plumage develops which remains until the end of October, or even early November in some mild autumns. Then the bird assumes its winter plumage, white all over save for a black tail and a red line over the eye. The male has an additional black line which appears to run through the eye. Plumage even covers the legs and feet, helping to cut down heat loss, an important consideration for a bird of the highlands where winters are long and hard. Bilberry, crowberry, and to a lesser extent heather, form the bulk of its food, which may have to be unearthed, by foot, from beneath a carpet of snow.

A great deal of research has been carried out on *Lagopus mutus* in an effort to discover the precise external stimulus that sets off the change into white plumage. Temperature seems to be the main factor, although the suggestion that day-length has nothing to do with it is probably wrong. The moult is initiated when the average temperature falls to about 4.5 °C and is complete by the time this has fallen a further 7 °C to about −3 °C. This may not be until November in

Scotland, but further north, in the Arctic proper, may be as early as September.

In Britain, three mountain species — the ptarmigan, the snow bunting and the dotterel — can be regarded as survivors of the bird life which flourished soon after the last glaciation relaxed its steely grip. Both the dotterel and the snow bunting hang on to their breeding status, the dotterel just, the snow bunting rather better of late. In winter it flocks around the skiers' picnic sites like sparrows. The ptarmigan is by far the most numerous of this select group in the highlands of Scotland, and the population probably exceeds 25,000 birds. It is, however, absent from lowland areas — and from Ireland, where it is replaced by the red grouse. The next time you are wiping the snow from your eyes or de-icing your car, remember that the ptarmigan, that 13 inch (35 centimetre) bundle of feathers, finds it much too warm for comfort at low levels.

At the top of every food pyramid is an arch-predator. Because these efficient hunters are thought to present a threat to man or his live-stock they are often accused of deeds they do not commit, and attempts, often successful, are made to eradicate them. A look at a map of any upland area of Britain will reveal evocatively named spots such as Eagle Crag, Eagle Rock and so on. The proud birds once seen on these lofty perches have now gone; the golden eagle has struggled for survival. Indeed it is still struggling, but with man's more enlightened attitude of recent years, there are signs that it may once again soar splendidly over the moors of England and Wales.

> He clasps the crag with crooked hands;
> Close to the sun in lonely lands,
> Ring'd with the azure world, he stands.
>
> The wrinkled sea beneath him crawls;
> He watches from his mountain walls,
> And like a thunderbolt he falls.

Tennyson's lines on 'The Eagle' give the impression of a fierce, dominating bird frightened of nothing. In fact the reverse is true, and the great birds quickly and quietly desert their nests if regularly disturbed. This feature of their behaviour is as big a threat to their continued survival in Britain as actual egg-collecting, or breeding failure for some other reason. Nowhere is this more apparent than in the Lake District. Two days after their eyrie was pinpointed in a newspaper article, a pair of birds had over 90 'ornithologists' creeping towards them. They must be given peace if they are to thrive. Their present population in Britain as a whole must be regarded as reasonably healthy, having survived widespread persecution throughout the nineteenth century; the *Atlas of Breeding Birds in*

Golden eagle

Britain and Ireland puts the figure at between 250 and 300 pairs. But apart from the odd pair in the Lake District, golden eagles are restricted to Scotland, where the situation is not too satisfactory. The RSPB, in their publication *The Hidden Killers*, point out that some misguided landowners are still laying down poisoned baits for birds of prey on moorlands on which they wish to shoot grouse. And 'For wheresoever the carcase is, there will the eagles be gathered together,' as the New Testament records! Eagles are never slow to take carrion. It cannot be denied that the diet of the golden eagle does include grouse, as well as hare and ptarmigan, but this is no excuse; the eagle is protected by law.

The eyrie is constructed of sticks, perhaps in an isolated Scots pine but more probably on a rocky mountain face. For the whole time the two or more eggs are being incubated fresh nesting material is added. Usually all the eggs in the clutch hatch, but more often than not only one youngster is successfully fledged. Pliny provided one explanation:

> Before its young are as yet fledged, the eagle compels them to gaze at the rays of the sun, and if it observes one to wink or show a watery eye, casts it from the nest as a degenerate offspring; if, on the contrary, it preserves a steady gaze it is saved from this hard fate, and brought up.

What actually happens to the youngest chick is much more rational. The female lays her eggs at three- or often four-day intervals, which means that one chick is always stronger than any of the others. In times of food shortage the larger eaglet consumes the smaller. This is of great survival value to the species, since it enables one eaglet to survive, rather than all perishing; sentiment is a word unknown in nature. The eaglets are initially covered with an attractive white down which is gradually moulted and replaced by a mottled brown plumage. After twelve weeks or so another eagle soars high over the highlands. Long may we allow them to do so.

Thus we have examined just a little of the wildlife of our upland regions and have seen the threats it faces. Once again provision must be made for those who wish to watch and above all for those who are being watched.

7
The Coastline

The seacoast of Britain is one of the most beautiful in the world; but it has the problem that none of us lives more than 90 miles from it. Many of our rivers have carried shipping for centuries and around their estuaries have sprung up huge ports with their associated industries, bringing pollution and squalor. Again man's increasing leisure and his desire to spend it in pleasant places is putting strain on the environment. Coastal wildlife once more is subject to the two modern evils, disturbance and pollution.

The estuarine environment, where the country meets the sea, can be a rich habitat for wildlife watchers. So can salt marshes and sand dunes, both of them areas slow to form and easy to destroy. The rich salt marshes are coveted by industrialists and farming communities whilst sand dunes attract holidaymakers by the thousand. Rare plants including helleborines and sea bindweed are gathered by eager children, and plants which serve to bind the dunes are dug up by others constructing sandcastles. But as we have seen in previous chapters it is often more difficult to recognise a problem than it is to solve it.

Estuaries

On the principle that all liquids allowed to run freely find their own level, all upland water either evaporates or eventually reaches the sea. The current will still be strong enough to transport suspended matter, often very rich in nutrients, at least until it meets tidal forces. Where they clash, the two forces cancel each other out and the rich solids are deposited. The main area of deposition is the estuary, and if the rich food base so provided was the only factor to be considered then the creatures living here would find few problems. However, estuarine organisms need to find a way of living in a salinity which varies from hour to hour, day to day and season to season. Molluscs, crustaceans, annelid worms and a host of others do this successfully, inhabiting

Shelduck

estuaries in vast numbers, making rich pickings for the birds. Prominent among these is the shelduck, which can be seen on the open mudflats sweeping its head from side to side as it feeds on quantities of a tiny estuarine snail called *Hydrobia*. It is the wading birds, however, that tend to dominate the enormous areas of mudflats exposed when the tide is out. Huge populations of knot and dunlin, redshanks, oystercatchers and curlews occur, along with smaller numbers of sanderling, godwits, turnstones and ringed plovers. One's first impression on looking at this mass of birds is that they are all competing with each other to find enough food to stay alive. An important biological principle states that no two species can share the same habitat and consume identical food — have an identical biological niche — without one being slightly more efficient than the other; gradually the less favoured species will become rarer and might eventually become extinct. Waders avoid direct competition by having evolved legs of different lengths, which allow some to wade deeper than others, and bills of varying lengths and shapes, allowing them to penetrate the rich mud to different depths. To some extent also, different species, or different-size categories within a species, of mud-dwelling animals have evolved to live at varying depths, establishing their unique ecological niches; so each species of wader can feed on a separate invertebrate with very little overlap. Competition is reduced to a minimum and survival for all is possible.

187

Digging for lugworms to use for bait at Morecambe Bay

At this moment, however, these food-rich estuaries are more vulnerable than any other environment — and this is saying something. Over 30 per cent of the population of these islands lives close to estuaries. Great demands are being made for land to be reclaimed for factories, farmland, housing and holiday complexes of one sort or another. Discharge of sewage, including large quantities of chemicals and hot water, into estuaries from these large conurbations is an obvious problem, but the more subtle aspects can be harder to overcome. For example, the effects of tipping liquids containing large amounts of suspended solids into estuarine waters (or any other waters for that matter) are further-reaching than we knew until recently. The tiny green plants (phytoplankton) which manufacture food by photosynthesis may then be denied the light essential to the process, and so the food pyramid collapses at its base. The cleaner the water the further the light can penetrate and the greater the potential volume of phytoplankton. Even a non-toxic chemical can cloud the water enough to destroy life altogether.

Low tide at Looe, Cornwall

Oil pollution has been with us as long as crude fuel has been transported by sea and tankers have found it cheaper to clean out their tanks at sea to save turn-round time. In 1922 Britain was the first country in the world to pass an Act preventing the discharge of oil into her territorial waters. The law did not work then and others like it do not work now. The Royal Society for the Protection of Birds have vehemently expressed disquiet and pointed out that the massive increase in the oil being taken from the North Sea must threaten our seabird colonies as they have never been threatened before. In 1979 the Society produced a seven-point plan which if heeded could do much to ease the threat. They ask for:

1 An extension of the present three-mile limit of our coastal waters to 12 miles, enlarging our area of jurisdiction over foreign vessels;

2 Joint action by EEC coastal states against oil pollution, off western Europe in particular;

3 Better policing of the seas so that 'pirate' ships discharging oil can be detected and fined heavily;

4 Prevention of pollution from routine discharge of oil, including fuel oil, from all classes of ship — a major cause of bird deaths;

5 A halt on further oil exploration and production in inshore areas of outstanding wildlife importance until oil pollution prevention and clean-up methods provide adequate safeguards:

6 A big increase in research and development of clean-up technology;

7 A 'fighting fund' raised by a levy on the oil and shipping industries to pay for the clean-up of spills whose source is unknown.

Pollution is always with us but on occasion the effects can be more severe than usual, and the issue then becomes headline news. Sensational headlines, however, only work once or twice. The fuss dies down, and in the eyes of the general public the problem has been solved. It has not gone away, however, merely satisfied the media's thirst for a good story. The sooner this problem is tackled at the highest level and at whatever cost, the better it will be for ourselves, but more importantly for future generations.

Any form of pollution must be carefully monitored. A huge bird population winters on the estuary of the Mersey, for example, and during the autumn and winter of 1979–80 significant numbers of birds perished, including teal, pintail, mallard, shelduck, redshank, curlew, dunlin and knot. What caused these deaths was probably the combined effect of several poisonous materials, but most of the corpses examined had high levels of lead in their kidneys. It should be remembered that the birds dying are often at the apex of their food pyramid — a position which we ourselves occupy in our own pyramid.

The form of pollution that can be guaranteed to create the greatest

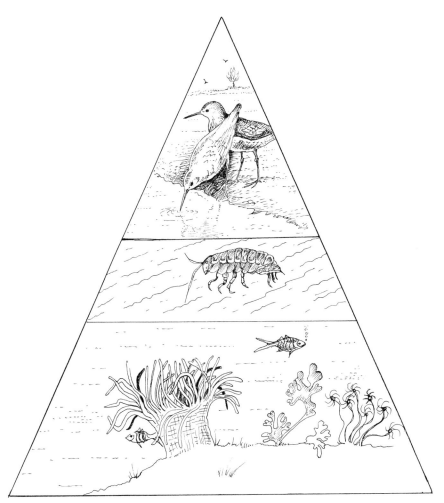

Food pyramid for sea with phytoplankton, shrimp and wading birds

outcry is that caused by the radionucleotides Strontium 90, Caesium 13 and Rubidium 106. Nuclear power stations tend to be sited on coasts close to estuaries so that their discharges can be carried out to sea. Significant traces of these pollutants have been found in the tissues of fish, even those caught far away from coasts. The effects of these on the human race may well be long-term, but they need watching.

In one aspect of pollution above all others the work of amateur natural historians could well be of more use than professional research. Anyone who has watched his or her own little area for many years will be aware of what is normal and what is not. Abnormally low populations of a particular species will be obvious to the local amateur,

191

Guillemot: threatened by oil pollution like the rest of the auks

but perhaps not to the visiting professional. This underlines the importance of many of us keeping a diary of apparently insignificant happenings on our own little patch: if we see the pattern changing and feel that all is not well, then we must make our voices heard. The problem of cleaning up our estuaries is more important than building motorway complexes, than supporting food mountains to sell at a loss, than local government expenditure, even more vital than education: it is life itself, to a country with such an extensive and vulnerable coastline as Britain.

Salt Marshes

Left to its own devices the sea batters away the land at one point but the erosion is counter-balanced by deposition at another. As the mineral-rich deposits carried by the rivers fall out of suspension, part of the estuary silts up and eventually becomes an area of salt marsh.

Pintail

These are fascinating places for the naturalist but they also attract the eye of farmers and industrialists — often one and the same these days. The wildlife of the salt marshes is under threat. Just what is there to lose?

Salt-marsh Plants
As it combines features of both the marine and the terrestrial zones, the botanical list is extensive, including many species uniquely adapted to the special conditions of this habitat. Plants here must cope with the problem of total or partial immersion in salt water which would tend to suck normal plants dry by osmosis (the movement of water from a weak solution to a stronger solution through a living membrane). Many salt-marsh plants, the halophytes, have therefore evolved thick, fleshy skins and strong cell sap, among other strategies — not unlike those of desert succulents — to cope with life in this salty habitat.

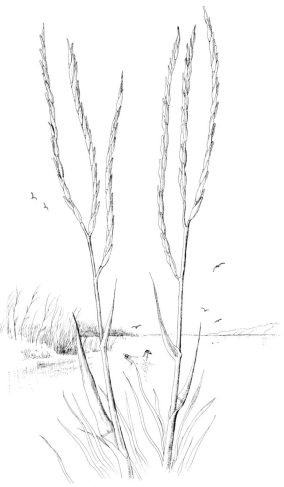

Rice grass

Rice grass (*Spartina townsendii*) is a hybrid between common cord grass (*Spartina maritima*), which is native to Britain, and a North American species noted near Southampton in 1829 and called *Spartina alterniflora*. The hybrid displays another example of the hybrid vigour mentioned in Chapter 1; from its first being noticed in 1879 its spread has been incredible. Its preferred habitat is sloppy mud, which it quickly binds together, making the habitat more suitable for other less vigorous plants. Indeed it often takes over completely, outstripping slower colonies like glasswort and sea aster. It thus plays a valuable role in consolidating and raising marsh levels, though in some places its sheer dynamism is a matter of concern to those interested in maintaining a diverse salt-marsh flora. It often grows to a metre high and flowers from July to October.

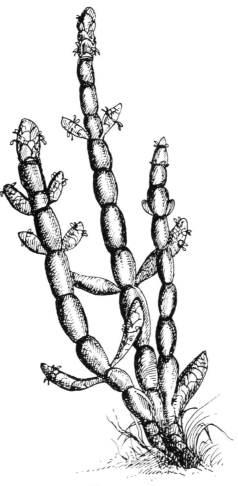

Glasswort

Glasswort (*Salicornia europaea agg*) has many alternative names including marsh samphire. A member of the goosefoot family, it grows well on wet mud and is a true pioneer species. The predominant colour is green but it is often tinged with red. It used to be collected and burned to produce soda, which in turn was used in the manufacture of glass. In some coastal areas the succulent samphire with its candelabra of shoots is still collected and served as a pickle, especially with meat. It flowers from July to September.

The lovely sea lavender (*Limonium vulgare*) is found in the central areas of many salt marshes and in July and August it can be quite dominant, especially in areas where there is little grazing by sheep. Its origins are south European; it does not thrive in Scotland and has not reached Ireland at all. It does have some scent, but this is not nearly as

Sea lavender

Sea aster

powerful as that of the common lavender. The plant is perennial and the flowers grow to a height of between 6 inches and one foot (15 to 30 centimetres). Sea aster (*Aster tripolium*) joins in the colonising process a bit further up the marsh from glasswort, and often in association with sea lavender. It is a handsome bluish-coloured member of the daisy family (Compositae), with a long and interesting history. In Elizabethan times Gerard recommended the roots as a treatment for dropsy, an antidote to poisons and an ointment for the healing of wounds. It was transplanted into the gardens of the herbalists, where it survived for a time, but could not be cultivated effectively. It was called Michaelmas daisy at this time; the garden plant which now bears this vernacular name is similar in appearance to sea aster but is actually *Aster paniculatus*, introduced from the New World about 1600.

Thrift

In contrast to the sea aster, the familiar thrift (*Armeria maritima*) transplants well and is grown in gardens. It occurs at the top of salt marshes, lining shingle ridges, but is seen at its best on sea cliffs; it also grows on rocky and mountainous places inland. Thrift grows from a rosette of fleshy — halophytic — leaves. The stalks are leafless and support a globular head of pink flowers anything up to 6 inches (15 centimetres) above the ground. A close look with a magnifying glass will reveal that each tiny flower has five petals and five sepals. It has many vernacular names, including sea pink, lady's pincushion, cushion pink and sea daisy. It does not seem to have had any medicinal significance but its symmetrical beauty was acknowledged by its portrait appearing on the reverse side of the twelve-sided threepenny piece minted during the reign of George VI.

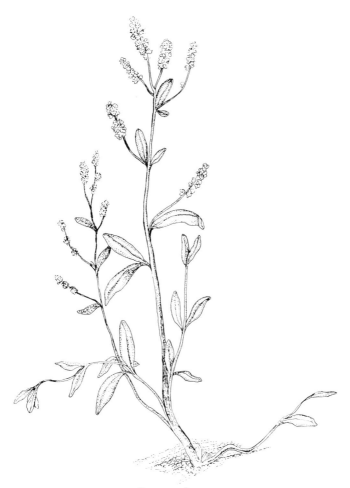

Sea purslane

Sea purslane (*Halimione portulacoides*) is not spectacular but dominates part of the salt marshes. It thrives best on the well-drained edges, and is typically found on the banks of ditches formed where the bulk of the silt has been deposited. This species is particularly common on the east coast; in his book *Flowers of the Coast* Ian Hepburn defines its northerly limit as a line drawn diagonally from Berwick on the east coast to the Duddon estuary on the west. On the Duddon estuary, sea purslane is indeed a dominant plant in many of its salt marshes, as well as being found further north. It is a low shrubby perennial with straggly, branching stems, silvery-grey leaves, and insignificant yellowish flowers which can be found from July to October.

The leaves of sea plantain (*Plantago maritima*), which often dominates salt marshes, sometimes out-competing thrift and sea lavender, are so favoured by sheep that in North Wales it has been deliberately cultivated for their benefit. It is a perennial with long, narrow, succulent leaves, its green flowers on a thin cylindrical spike carried from June to September; the yellow pollen-laden anthers contrast sharply with the green to make this a most attractive plant.

Salt-marsh Birds and Animals

Just as the forest edge is an especially rich habitat, so the salt marsh, bordering land and sea, is highly productive, attracting a great variety of birds to feed there. In winter, brent geese specialise on the sea-flowering eel-grass (*Zostera*). A heavy crop of energy-rich seeds in the late summer and autumn attracts large flocks of migrant birds; hungry linnets, greenfinches and yellow-hammers cover the saltings, their flight calls reverberating in the air. These attract some interesting predators, including the tiny killer the merlin, the slow-flapping but lethal short-eared owl, that skilful flier the hen harrier, and the peregrine, a sort of flying slaughter-house. The balance of nature is often subtly maintained, but life on the salt marsh can show the red-in-tooth-and-claw aspect extremely clearly.

During the winter the temperature in these salt-laden areas will be higher than inland and creatures dependent upon open stretches of fresh water may be forced to move to the coast when their usual haunts are frozen over. During the winter of 1979, in a house overlooking the Duddon estuary, I was watching a scattered flock of feeding redshanks through a haze of sea mist and noticed what seemed to be two black retrievers swimming on an ebbing tide. One of them dived and surfaced gripping a protesting flat fish tight in its jaws and hauled out onto an uncovered mudbank. The mist lifted a little and I focused my binoculars not on a dog, but upon a splendid otter, which was soon joined by the second animal. I was delighted to see them, because if any British mammal is staring extinction in the face it must surely be the otter (*Lutra lutra*).

> I am a bold otter as you'll hear,
> And I've rambled the country all round.
> I value no dogs far and near,
> In the water nay yet on the ground.
> Well I value no dogs far and near,
> But I rove through the country so wide,
> Till I come to the river so clear,
> That did Clifton and Prestwich divide.

This is the first verse of a mid-eighteenth-century hunting song, based on the River Irwell near Manchester. It was recently revived by folk-singer Harry Boardman. Obviously the otter is not found anywhere near the Irwell these days. Its range has contracted

Otters

alarmingly and heavy coastal pollution could be a stumbling block to its recovery just when many of our rivers are improving. Reduction of suitable habitat, polluted waters and otter hunting, probably in that order, have been responsible for its present-day plight. The long-overdue protection was given from January 1978, when the otter was added to Schedule I of animals protected under the 1975 Conservation of Wild Creatures and Wild Plants Act, but it should be noted that this only applies to England and Wales and not to Scotland where otters are described — somewhat optimistically — as common. In fact it is only in remote highland areas and offshore islands that they are found in any numbers. In England and Wales the legislation may have come too late. Must we wait for otters inhabiting the Scottish lochs, rivers and estuaries to decline before we protect them? There is another even more worrying feature, now that hunting the otter is banned in England and Wales. When the packs were hunting otters, they occasionally flushed a mink and hunted it because the hounds could not be stopped. Many packs have now decided to try to help the cause of conservation by controlling the population of mink. What

happens if they flush an otter whilst hunting the mink? You know, I know and the hunters know; but does the Government know? It does and something must be done about it. This loophole must be closed, or this delightful beast will be, like the wolf, the beaver, the boar and the bear, literally a part of our natural *history*.

Sand Dunes

Sand dunes are formed when sand is driven by prevailing winds until it reaches an obstruction. This can be shingle or a piece of driftwood but it is sometimes a very tough flowering plant such as prickly saltwort (*Salsola kali*), sea rocket (*Cakile maritima*) or even glasswort (*Salicornia europaea*). When the plant dies, the level of sand increases and the plant bodies are incorporated, serving to enrich the nutrient-deficient sand. Thus the habitat becomes suitable for the growth of much more binding grasses, such as lyme grass (*Elymus arenarius*), sand couch grass (*Agropyron junceiforme*), and sea couch grass (*Agropyron pungens*), but not yet for the marram grass (*Ammophila arenaria*). Unlike the couches, which can withstand inundation by the sea, marram cannot tolerate being splashed by salt spray. But once other vegetation has raised the height of the sandhills sufficiently to protect it, marram is the most important stabiliser of dunes. All sand-dune plants have to adapt to living in areas where the supply of fresh water is limited and have evolved various strategies to deal with this problem. They are therefore called xerophytes (Greek *xeros*, dry, *phytos*, plant).

Marram has two major specialised features. It is through the pores, or stomata, on plant leaves that water is lost by transpiration and respiratory gases enter and leave. In marram the stomata are situated on the lower surface of the leaf, which is inrolled during dry weather, forming a tube; the air within it becomes saturated and no more water is lost. Then, the underground stems with attached roots spread far and wide, serving the dual function of trapping water and binding the plant firmly to the soil. Yet another adaptive feature is its ability to accelerate its growth when buried by sand.

Amongst the extensive tufts of marram other specialised plants can survive, including sand spurge (*Euphorbia paralias*), lady's bedstraw (*Galium verum*) and the fascinating sea holly (*Eryngium maritimum*). 'Let the sky rain potatoes; let it thunder to the tune of "Greensleeves", hail kissing-comfits and snow eringoes,' quoth the fat gourmet Sir John Falstaff in Shakespeare's *Merry Wives of Windsor*, and by 'eringoes' he meant the roots of sea holly soaked and candied in honey

Marram grass

Sea holly

or some other sugary solution. At one time the sale of eringoes was a flourishing trade centred around Colchester in Essex, where it only disappeared about 1870. This plant is no relation to the holly (*Ilex aquifolium*), although its leaves are remarkably similar in shape. Sea holly, with its attractive greyish-green leaves and bluish flowers, is a member of the Umbelliferae.

Even when marram has taken hold, a young dune is still distinctly unstable and high winds can punch huge holes in the sandhills — a blow-out. However, as more plants colonise and bind the sand, the dune becomes increasingly less mobile. A new 'embryo' dune may start building seaward of it, giving added protection from the wind and accelerating the stabilising process of the more landward dunes.

Gradually the dead, decaying plants add weight and fertility to the sand and a rich soil accumulates. The dune is now said to be fixed, and an impressive flora develops, including burnet rose (*Rosa pimpinellifolia*), heartsease pansy (*Viola tricolor*), harebell (*Campanula rotundifolia*), thyme (*Thymus serpyllum*), yellow rattle (*Rhinanthus*

A blow-out

A developing dune system — the Lots Beach, Askam-in-Furness, Cumbria

minor), hare's-foot clover (*Trifolium arvense*) and the evocative-sounding rest harrow (*Ononis spinosa*). The land at this stage may truly be said to have been reclaimed from the sea.

The rest harrow's roots may well have resisted the passage of primitive agricultural machinery. It also had two other names, equally descriptive: *resta-bovis*, which literally meant an ox-stop, and *remora aratri*, which translates as plough-arrester. The old-time farmers had another reason for disliking it, since if cattle ate it they tended to produce tainted milk. The children had more affection for this plant with the delicate pink pea-like flowers: they used to dig up the roots, chew them and call them wild liquorice. Sometimes the roots were shaken up with water and called 'Spanish juice'. I've drunk many a gallon of this stuff as a youngster brought up in maritime Cumbria.

Dune systems, like the mountain-top tundra discussed in the last chapter, take a long time to develop (an estimated 300 years at Scolt Head in Norfolk) and are easily destabilised. If a rabbit burrow can lead to the collapse of a dune ridge and a blow-out, how vulnerable they are to the tramping of human feet. Excessive human traffic can cause even quite elaborate dunes to disappear with startling rapidity, taking their unique flora with them. Sea holly, for example, was once common all round the British Isles, but human encroachment has made it rare in the north and east, and it continues to decline elsewhere. A human picnic party is one of the least controllable phenomena on earth, and short of sectioning off choice parts of the coast as nature reserves, there seems little hope of the situation improving.

Within the fixed dunes there are often damp hollows with their own characteristic flora and fauna. They are called slacks, a word which derives directly from the old Norse word *slakki*, a damp valley. I have made a special study of these areas and the many plants growing there include marsh orchis (*Dactylorhiza incarnata*), marsh helleborine (*Epipactis palustris*), marsh cinquefoil (*Potentilla palustris*), grass of Parnassus (*Parnassia palustris*) and meadowsweet (*Filipendula ulmaria*). These dune slacks are of course lost when land is taken over to build bungalows and caravan sites. Some steps, however, are being taken to preserve them. One of the animals found here is, like the otter, included in Schedule I of animals protected under the 1975 Conservation of Wild Creatures and Wild Plants Act. This is the natterjack toad and with the strength of British law behind it the creature should be safe. Yet one of my own favourite natterjack areas was threatened, not by an individual but by the council representing the town of Millom in Cumbria. They were proposing to drain a natterjack pool in order to build a caravan site. 'Commercial development should be maintained at all costs,' declared the county council. They also said:

Unfortunately the lagoon is one of the few remaining breeding sites of the Natterjack toad. And the Natterjack is listed on the schedule of the Conservation of Wild Creatures and Wild Plants Act. This provides for fines of £200 against people disturbing the species listed.

A council member is reported as making one of the most irresponsible statements ever uttered on an environmental subject: 'A council spokesman said that they were aware of the law but felt that tourist development should take precedence over conservation.' This is tantamount to saying that if the fine is less than the potential profit, then the law must be broken. The council, however, cynically shifted the responsibility, adding: 'Ultimately, however, it will be the developer of the site who will have to decide whether or not to break the law.' It seems, then, that laws to protect our wild things are sometimes ignored by the responsible people we have elected to preserve them for ourselves, and for our children.

The scientific name for the rare natterjack toad (*Bufo calamita*)

Natterjack toad

seems apt, for *calamita* conveys the word for its present status! The word natterjack has an interesting derivation, from two Old English words, 'nether' meaning low-lying, and 'jack', meaning tiny. This little animal, about 2¾ inches (70mm) long, and 3¼ inches (80mm) for the female, has given me so many enjoyable hours watching it running about the dunes and spawning in the slacks. The species is easily distinguished by a yellow line which runs down the middle of its back and by the fact that it does not hop like a common toad, but runs quickly, as befits a very active animal. Indeed one of its popular vernacular names is the running toad.

In the main the natterjack is nocturnal and spends the day in a tunnel burrowed in the sand by its forelimbs, the more powerful pair. The breeding season can commence in mid-April and is often still in progress at the end of June or even early in July. The spawn is laid in strings up to 6 feet (2m) long and containing 3–4,000 eggs each of about 1/10 inch (1.5mm) in diameter. They hatch sometime between the fifth and the tenth day, the precise timing depending upon the temperature. The whole metamorphosis takes only 6–8 weeks, which is very fast when compared to the development of the common frog (*Rana temporaria*) which can take as long as 14 weeks and the common toad which takes from 8 to 12 weeks. The accelerated growth of the natterjack is thought to be a safety device to avoid mortality caused by the shallow pools in the dune slacks drying up during late summer. Low-lying tiny Jack is not able to remain active during the rigours of a British winter and hibernates, often in groups, from October until late February or early March.

Beyond the natterjack dunes lies the open beach, often covered in shingle. This is the favourite habitat of one of our rarest seabirds, the little tern (*Sterna albifrons*). This bird is another creature battling against the odds in modern Britain, nesting as it does on shingle and sandy beaches, a habitat also enjoyed by man. The summer sunbathers often fail to realise that they are close to a tern's nest and are preventing the return of the incubating bird. Without the shade of the adult's body the egg and its developing embryo will literally boil.

Sea angling is another enjoyable and rapidly expanding hobby; the fisherman hurling his expectant line seawards into the cool wind and rain we often get even in July does not notice the three camouflaged tern eggs close to his feet. This time the eggs are needing the warmth of the parent's body and are likely to perish for want of it. We should be pleased that the sunworshippers and the fishermen have the leisure to indulge in their chosen hobbies. But what can we do to help the beautiful little tern to co-exist?

Extensive field studies by the RSPB have shown the success of full-time wardening in protecting little tern colonies from human disturbance, including egg collectors. All surviving Welsh-coast colonies, for instance, are now fully wardened in the breeding season and numbers have slowly built up in some. To give some idea of the pressures the terns face, a single pair at Gwynedd was disturbed no less than 535 times in 41 days, with humans and gulls the chief offenders. Fences prevented fatally close encroachment, however, and the pair still managed to raise two chicks. Throughout Britain, hundreds of leaflets have been handed out to holidaymakers explaining the reasons for restricted access. Wardens report that the welfare of the terns often becomes a matter of local civic pride, and a regular topic of conversation in shops and camp sites.

Over the last century the fortunes of *Sterna albifrons* have fluctuated. A low ebb was reached in Britain and Ireland during the nineteenth century, but by 1930 a distinct improvement had taken place to over 3,000 pairs. Since then the population has declined almost by half, to about 1,800 breeding pairs; this is a low figure but the decline seems to have been halted there for the time being. The little tern probably ranks as third rarest of our seabirds, behind the Arctic skua

Little tern

and the roseate tern. In other parts of its range it is not rare, and if we provide this, the smallest of our terns, with just a little protection at the right time then it will not be lost to Britain.

Thus we have seen some of the organisms struggling to survive on our crowded coastlines the sandy parts of which, at least, are so vulnerable to ill-treatment of one sort or another. The question is not can the wildlife survive this onslaught, but how we can ensure that it does. More coastal reserves with limited access must be set up and the areas of coast under the control of the Ministry of Defence must be maintained and monitored by ecologists. The real answer to the problem, however, lies in education: firstly education of those who use our estuaries for business, including the heedless captains of large tankers who flush clean their oily tanks at sea, and secondly education of the people who come from our urban jungles to the seaside to enjoy themselves. Posters urging people to protect the wildlife and printing the country code in the seaside-town guides could do nothing but good.

The local public relations campaigns mounted to enlist support for little-tern protection show what can be done, and how responsive people are if approached in the right way, told about the problem and asked to help. Schools have a valuable part to play here, and surprisingly many lessons can be learned right on the doorstep, even in town schools. Urban wildlife is quite capable of looking after itself, and well worth the trouble of getting to know.

8
Urban Wildlife

Wildlife in its varied forms has continuously adjusted to man's exploitation. Against the primitive natural condition, continuous belts of undisturbed forest, we now have a fragmented, highly artificial environment, designed to our needs, round the modern city, with its ever-present ancillaries — the transportation network and waste-disposal systems. Opportunist plants and animals have turned even these to their advantage in unexpected ways. If some colonisation can be achieved here, how much more might we hope of our parks and gardens? While they are a far cry from ancient forest, they have certain great advantages; after all their mosaic lay-out combines certain attributes of both forest and field, and we might expect some of the best of both worlds, just as we have found with the forest edge, hedgerow and salt marsh. We now have exotic invaders, accidental or otherwise, for in this age of global travel flora and fauna are much less exclusive to their countries of origin. When these exotics slot in nicely they are an asset, but just as often they flourish at the expense of a well-loved native species. In all, we find that notwithstanding the intensity of urban life, a city can and does support a remarkable complexity of wildlife, with opportunities for ecological management and education almost as interesting as those of a primeval forest! We must recognise the city as a valid, if bizarre, habitat in its own right.

Roads

Both Palaeolithic and Mesolithic man engaged in trade much more than we might think. Recognised routes through the forests were in use, following the tracks of meandering animals which had trampled down the vegetation and made man's progress easier. These routes often advanced on a wide front, funnelling to a narrow track only when approaching shallow stretches of watercourses. If they fell into disuse they quickly became overgrown. Feeding animals do not move in straight lines and some of these tracks were far from direct.

Motorway under construction — M65 Colne to Blackburn

It was the Romans who first made road building into a construction industry; but without sophisticated machinery little, if any, damage would be done to the environment. This remained the case until modern times, the roads assisting rather than threatening our wildlife. However, from the time of Macadam onwards, culminating in our present motorway system, nature has faced a serious challenge. The initial effect of a new motorway on the environment through which it forces its way is catastrophic. Let us not attempt to hide the horror. Nature, however, is eventually more than a match for man and a motorway verge can develop into a long thin nature reserve, seldom if ever visited by man and therefore a private place.

The wildlife is learning not to venture on to the road, but could face another danger more subtle but just as deadly. This is 'heavy metal' poisoning, caused especially by lead, which could arise from the high levels released in the exhaust fumes of vehicles. The fall-out, however, seems to be over a short distance (two metres or so) and only the areas very close to the hard shoulder should be affected — a tatty area anyway, littered with rubber from blow-outs. One thing which the government could profitably do is to make financial provision for a conservation officer to be responsible for monitoring the wildlife on each motorway. What a splendid title — Nature Warden for the M5!

In the early 1970s the Nature Conservancy surveyed the plants

Long-tailed fieldmouse

growing on the verges of the M1 between Leeds and Hendon. The original contractors had sown the areas with four species of grass and clover in 1959, the year of the motorway's completion. The seventies' survey found nearly 400 species of plants! Some motorway verges, and especially central reservations, have proved such quiet retreats (in terms of lack of herbicides and interruptions by heavy feet, not of decibels) that they have been planted with rare plants in the hope that a reservoir of our wild heritage will be maintained.

Where vegetation thrives in Britain one will always find small mammals, and on the verges and the central reservations they live in huge numbers. Perhaps the slight warmth generated by the vehicles may be some advantage to their energy budget. Two particularly common species are the long-tailed field mouse and the short-tailed field vole. One recent suggestion is that the rodent population in the centre reservation of a motorway system may exceed the number of vehicles at rush hour. This may explain the regular sight of kestrels hovering to hunt over the verges.

The ground close to the motorway is well drained and can support a

Harvest mouse, another motorway — verge inhabitant

high population of earthworms. Many birds, including lapwings, golden plovers, black-headed gulls, carrion crows, rooks and starlings, seem to feed in fields close to busy roads. This could be due to the fact that the vibrations generated by traffic cause worms to surface to see if it is raining. Thus the lapwing has a sort of 'artificial pattering system', similar to the natural one discussed in Chapter 4. It is interesting to notice that once they have fed, the birds gain height prior to crossing the road, although many young, naïve rooks in particular, get run over in the summer months.

Road designers used to be inclined to build first and explain what they had done later. They still do not talk to conservationists enough, but at least they do talk. As a result of sensible debate, underpasses for badgers have been constructed on some systems, including the M56 near Frodsham. Badgers need all the help they can get at the moment; electric railway lines have done them no good, and despite the passing of the 1974 Badger Protection Act, 'hunting the brock' with little dogs still continues, especially in remote country areas. Moreover until late 1979 wholesale gassing of badgers was carried out in south-western

Badger

England because the animal is 'suspected' of carrying bovine tuberculosis. How nice if one of our most ancient woodland mammals could settle down in peace in the middle of our newest road systems.

Canals

Unless one actually lived before the age of canal construction and witnessed the 'cuts' slashing their way through the country greenery the true significance of this form of transport can probably not be fully realised. Imagine appalling unmade roads, no railways, only a small number of rivers wide enough or deep enough to carry traffic, and all you have left is isolation.

Although the principle of building some sort of artificial waterway was not new — indeed the Fosse Dyke was gouged out in the 1120s — the heyday of canal construction in Britain did not come until the late eighteenth century, and did not last long, the railway system taking over. With a few exceptions, notably the Manchester Ship Canal constructed as late as the 1890s, canals fell into disuse and decay. However they could not be allowed to go completely untended, since a leaking canal is a threat to agricultural enterprises, not to mention dwelling houses. Likewise the compensation reservoirs built to house reserves of water for topping up canals during periods of hot weather had to be maintained, at least to some extent. Some reservoirs have a long history of multiple use; Foulridge Reservoir near Colne in

Pleasure boats on the Leeds to Liverpool Canal, Burnley

Lancashire is one, and with the nearby Whitemoor and Slipper Hill Reservoirs is a haven for aquatic wildlife. Impressive winter counts of wildfowl, including whooper, Bewick's and mute swans as well as a flock of over 100 Canada geese and substantial flocks of teal, wigeon, mallard, pochard and tufted duck, are regular. Goldeneye and goosanders are never numerous but occur every year, and occasionally the smew is recorded.

Lower Foulridge is also an interesting spot for the bird watcher but he must share it with anglers, who catch roach, bream, perch and pike. There is also a substantial boating club, and possibly because the name Foulridge can grate a little on the ear, the sailors refer to this stretch of water as Lake Burwains. Naturalist, angler and sailor live together in peace and harmony and substantial numbers of birds breed, including the great crested grebe, little grebe, coot, moorhen, kingfisher, mallard and mute swan. The surrounding reed beds are high and shelter the lovely water vole (*Arvicola terrestris*), one of my favourite mammals.

Of all the ridiculous names for an aquatic animal — *terrestris* indeed!! Much better would be *Arvicola amphibius brigantium* Thomas, named after the man who proposed it in 1928 when he described a specimen from Huddersfield in Yorkshire. Another name

Foulridge Reservoir

this delightful little beast is saddled with is water rat, but it is easily distinguished from a true rat by a quieter disposition and a much shorter tail, muzzle and ears. To the inexperienced naturalist the only sign of the water vole will probably be a 'plop' as it dives into the water and scuds away under the surface and out of sight. This particular species is the largest of the British voles, measuring just about 8 inches (20cm). Its diet is mainly vegetable, but it is not averse to grinding up the odd water snail or caddis-fly larva. There has been some debate concerning whether water voles hibernate and whether they are diurnal or nocturnal, and modern researches seem to have cleared up both these points. There is no true hibernation, although periods of snow and frost may keep the beast at home, the males venturing out more than the females at these times. As to the activity cycle the animal alternates periods of four hours' activity with a similar period of rest. Apart from the breeding season, the sexes remain apart and both hold territory, usually a stretch of bank, the male's being larger than the female's. Most females produce two litters — the first usually in May — each of about five young per litter in a nest, a ball of rushes, usually sited beneath the ground but occasionally in vegetation. In Britain water voles have been accused of damaging canal banks, osier

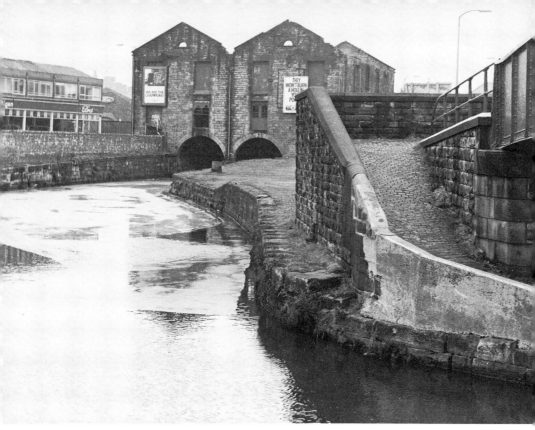

Wigan Pier

beds, and the willows used in the cricket-bat industry, but on balance this attractive mammal is neutral so far as man is concerned.

I have recorded the vole on many stretches of canal, perhaps the most bizarre spot being at Wigan Pier, on the Leeds to Liverpool. Conducting a survey here during the summer of 1979, I discovered twenty-five species of aquatic animal. Like the old music-hall comedians we do not realise that not only is Wigan quite beautiful in parts (like the curate's egg), but it actually has a pier. It not only dealt with commercial traffic, but had an organised passenger service, and at the turn of this century pleasure steamers ran excursions.

Railways

Britain in the nineteenth century was able to justify her boast of being the workshop of the world: smoke belched into her atmosphere, trees were felled as if there was no tomorrow, factories and their inhabitants groaned with effort. The existing transport systems failed to cope with new demand, and by the time of the Great Exhibition of 1851 the necessary technology had been developed and most of Britain's main towns were part of the railway network. Great scars had been gouged

Food pyramid for urban situations, with plants, mouse and badger

across our landscape. We may wonder if people objected to them then, as we do to motorway construction today — Wordsworth certainly did. To both the contemporary and the modern naturalist, the system has been a mixed blessing. The cuttings and tunnels made through the rocks led to great geological discoveries, which influenced Charles Darwin's thoughts on evolution. Fossilised seashells found on hilltops far inland clearly indicated two things, both highly contentious at the time. Firstly, the earth and the life forms upon it were of great antiquity, far older than the accepted 6,000 years or so suggested by Archbishop Usher who traced backwards the characters in the Bible to the time when Adam was a lad. Secondly, they clearly demonstrated that land masses were not static, but under constant stress, and vertical movements on a grand scale were taking place over time periods of equally unimagined length. Thus the pioneers of British Rail helped to advance man's biological thinking further in twenty years than it had moved in the previous twenty centuries.

On the other hand, great ecological damage was done, much of it by those who built the railways rather than by the engines that sped along the lines. The navvies who slaved, lived and died constructing tunnels and cuttings, burrowing under rivers and viaducting over them, created temporary havoc in the countryside through which they slowly passed. Once the steam trains were running, our wildlife had for the first time to cope with fast-moving inanimate objects, and huge numbers of animals must have perished. But again the plants began to colonise the raw and trampled areas, and then the animals above them in the food pyramid moved in. Springtime primroses yellowed the cuttings, wind-sown birch, hazel and alder began to offer food and shelter to the birds; rabbits and small rodents abounded. Life came back! In the days of coal-fed locomotives, sparks flew from the speeding snakes and at least the ash resulting from the embankment fires was a splendid fertiliser; pioneer species such as coltsfoot and ragwort did not miss the opportunity to fill the gap. Both these species are worth more than a casual glance.

Alder, a pioneer tree often found in new habitats

221

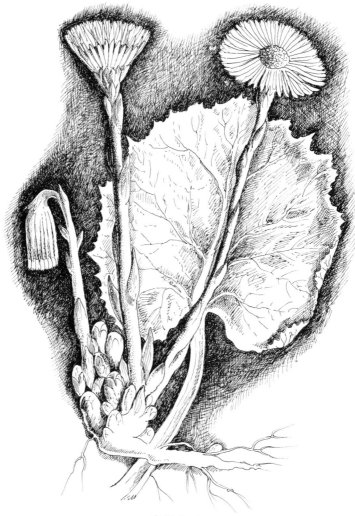

Coltsfoot

The vernacular name for coltsfoot (*Tussilago farfara*), a member of the Compositae family, derives from the shape of its large leaves which resemble the hoofprints of a horse; they appear after the more familiar yellow flowers, and are covered in light downy hairs. In the days before the invention of the match, these were scraped off, soaked in saltpetre and used in tinder-boxes. The scientific name *Tussilago* means 'cough' and comes from the plant's ancient function as a herb to cure chest complaints: its leaves were smoked as tobacco is smoked! The underground stems of the plant (the rhizomes) are still boiled in sugar and the resultant coltsfoot rock is sucked to relieve sore throats.

Ragwort (*Senecio jacobaea*) is also known as ragweed.

> Let Warlocks grim an' wither'd hags
> Tell how wi' you on ragweed nags
> They skim the muirs an' dizzy crags
> Wi' wicked speed.

Robert Burns was referring to ragwort's traditional function as a transport system for fairies — a sort of tourist-class broomstick. The spreading flower heads were also reputed to shelter the little people from heavy rain. In modern terms ragwort is seen as a pioneer species of waste spaces, the most important food plant for the larvae of the splendid-looking cinnabar moth and a nuisance on pastureland.

Cinnabar moth and ragwort

Cinnabar moth

The association between the cinnabar (*Callimorpha jacobaea*) and the ragwort can be seen from the specific name they share. The adult moths tend to become more active towards dusk, but are also seen during the day. The moth's red and black colouring is to us attactive, to birds the reverse, for this is one of nature's warning patterns. The moth is very bitter to the taste (oldtime naturalists tested them!) and even young birds try them but once. Yellow and black is a combination also ignored by predators and the equally distasteful cinnabar caterpillars which hatch from the shiny yellow eggs are banded in these colours. It has been suggested that the insatiable leaf-browsing of cinnabar-moth caterpillars might be used as an effective controlling agent for ragwort, which is sufficiently poisonous to affect cattle adversely and even taint their milk. Certainly numbers of them can shred a plant to the stem in no time. Interestingly, ragwort was introduced into New Zealand without the moth, and has become quite a problem in some places, lacking its usual controlling herbivore.

Disused railway — Colne to Barnoldswick

Cinnabar larvae are not totally dependent on ragwort; they will alternatively feed on coltsfoot, groundsel and a fascinating plant called Oxford ragwort.

It was in the environs of Oxford's Trinity College that Oxford ragwort (*Senecio squalidus*) first established itself in Britain. It came from plantings brought from Sicily and Italy (in the regions of Etna and Vesuvius) to the Botanic Gardens during the seventeenth century. By 1800 the alien was well established in the crannies of the college walls.

Then came the railways and this lover of disturbed ground had found its perfect ecological niche. It spread. The railway network has also been responsible for the rapid spread of many other species including ivy-leaved toadflax, yarrow, plantain, golden rod, Michaelmas daisy and buddleia. This latter species was brought in from China round about 1890 and has proved so attractive to butterflies that lepidopterists find that railway embankments where buddleia grows are amongst their most productive hunting grounds.

Working railways, however, are not areas around which to wander at will. Doctor Richard Beeching came to the rescue: during the early 1960s he pruned the railways to such an extent that thousands of miles of track were closed. So twenty years later we have quiet, overgrown nature reserves, abounding not only with native species of plant, but also with many exotic forms. Places of particular interest include the sites of the old station gardens, once tended with care by the railway staff, who often had a real pride in their job and the appearance of their working area. Exotic plants can be found growing close to sidings, which were parking areas for rolling stock bringing raw materials from various parts of the world. Nature has won — yet again.

Airports

When radar was in its infancy during Hitler's war the operators often had to try to interpret smudges and other ghostly apparitions which blurred their screens. They christened these 'angels' but it has since been firmly established that they were migrating birds. Valuable information on bird migration has since been gained from detailed radar studies. Altitude and airspeed can be calculated and such is the sophistication of modern electronics that the 'blips' on the screen can often be used to identify a definite species of bird. This information, however, has a disturbing side to it. The migrating birds are often sharing their flight paths with air traffic, and the danger of collision, with fearful loss of human life, is real. On 4 October 1960 a Lockheed Electric turbojet took off from Logan International Airport, Boston. Seconds after take-off it collided with a flock of starlings and crashed,

Brent goose

with the loss of 62 lives. The danger is always greater for jet aircraft, since the birds tend to get sucked into the turbos and thus destroy momentum. Nearly three-quarters of air strikes occur just before landing or just after take-off. One incident at Renfrew, in Scotland, for example, killed at least 400 gulls and caused almost £100,000 worth of damage to the aircraft, though by good luck no one was killed. Much research and money has gone, and is still going, into this problem. Surveys are done at prospective and existing sites, a multiple approach to bird-scaring is often employed, and ecology is taken into account: for example, by not leaving areas of short grass, attractive to roosting birds, and by siting airports away from reservoirs. Radar is used to predict large immigrant passages, especially of geese, and some information is exchanged at bird-strike conferences. This approach probably does not go far enough and more money is needed. It has been estimated for example that air strikes cost the RAF £1,200,000 per annum: what if ornithologists could save only 10 per cent of this sum? The need to consider bird life in the planning of new airports is now understood.

227

Britain's air traffic is increasing at nearly 20 per cent a year, so the demand for more and larger terminals will remain with us. Land is ever at a premium and London has already made a lecherous pass at the virgin areas of Sheppey and Foulness Island (Maplin). This seemed to the developers to be a logical choice — just an uninhabited area of sand and mud — a wasteland. But waste to whom? Certainly not to the hard-pressed wildlife of England's south-east. Conservationists objected with great force and for once put scientific objectivity first and dewy-eyed sentimentality second. This area in winter is home to nearly a quarter of a million birds, including 20 per cent of the world's population of dark-bellied brent geese. Even if the airport had been built the birds would not have lost their instinctive migratory urge and would have attempted to return. Imagine a collision between Concorde and a chevron of 1,000 brent geese. If for no other reason, this site should never have been considered; it now seems to have been dropped, at least for the moment. The world has four races of brent geese and two are European. These are the light-bellied brent (*Branta bernicla hrota*) and the dark-bellied brent (*Branta bernicla bernicla*), the race that winters at Foulness. These shore-loving geese are tough birds indeed, breeding on Russian tundra up to latitude 80°N, which is further north than any other species of goose can breed. On leaving their breeding grounds they resort to shallow sea coasts and estuaries of Germany, Holland, France and Great Britain, and a substantial proportion of the population come to Foulness in Essex. They feed on eel grass (*Zostera*) and marine green algae, and are strongly attached to traditional feeding areas. They fly reluctantly when disturbed and then usually at low altitude. Both these factors would spell great danger for both bird and aircraft close to an airport.

Sewage Farms

As already indicated sewage was, until the late nineteenth century, discharged directly into rivers. A treatment works was built at Reading in 1875 and other sewage-infested towns gradually followed suit. The solid matter is first removed and the less dense material is allowed to settle in lagoons. The liquid is aerated and then released into the watercourse, often after extensive and expensive treatment. The solid matter is spread out to decay and as it does so heat is generated, raising the local temperature and making sewage farms fairly hospitable for wildlife, especially in winter. Birds thrive there, feeding on invertebrates which abound in the sludge. Common species found include redshanks, lapwings, black-headed gulls, herring gulls, starlings and pied wagtails, but many other species come at times. At my local sewage works, for example, I have recorded 137 species in five

Duckpits sewage works, Burnley

years. The birds do have some problems, and occasionally become trapped in the evil sludge — a most unpleasant death.

Naturalists must never overlook the value of a study of a local sewage works — the smell is not so bad once you get used to it! Permission must always be obtained, but this is usually readily given. The rewards resulting from a visit are not only ornithological but often botanical. Many exotic fruits are eaten these days, and nature being what it is the seeds eventually arrive at the sludge lagoons, where they too find the comparatively high temperatures advantageous. More mundane plants found here include ox-eye daisy, many species of willowherb and nettles and their associated insects, and an interesting plant called mugwort (*Artemisia vulgaris*).

In days gone by this aromatic plant was thought to be a useful medicine. A perennial common throughout Britain it flowers late in summer until well into autumn. It may derive its vernacular name from the fact that it was used to provide a bitter taste to a mug of beer prior to the cultivation of the hop. It was known throughout Europe as a powerful plant; in pre-Christian times it was used in the 'Lay of the Nine Herbs' to protect against the venom of witchcraft transmitted through the air. Mugwort is the first plant mentioned.

> Have in mind Mugwort, what you made known
> What you laid down at the great denouncing
> Una your name is, oldest of herbs,
> Of might against thirty and against three
> Of might against venom, and the onflying
> Of might against the vile She who fares through the land.

229

Duckpits sewage works, Burnley

The medicinal values of the plant were still being expounded in the *Herbal Book* of 1867:

> Mugwort removes obstructions of urine caused by stone. A decoction is said to cure the Ague (Malaria). The Chinese use it to heal wounds applying the fresh plant bruised. A drachm of the leaves powdered was used to cure hysteric fits by Dr. Home. Made into an ointment with lard and a few daisies it was good for boils. Three drachms of the powder in wine is a speedy and certain remedy for sciatica. A decoction with camomile and agrimony and the place bathed while it is warm takes away the pains of the sinews and the cramp.

There is a Scots legend from Clydeside of a mermaid observing the funeral of a pretty maid and commenting:

> If they wad drink nettles in March
> And eat muggons in May,
> Sae mony braw maidens
> Wadna gang to the clay.

Here then is the cure-all — *and* it will flavour your beer!

Today's enormous volume of sewage is still causing problems, and

Mugwort

many modern treatment plants are, partly for aesthetic reasons, being sited underground. Obviously these are out of reach of the birds, and naturalists of the future may not find sewage works such happy hunting grounds. A glance through the literature of country bird clubs shows that a substantial percentage of rarities have been recorded actually within or very close to the perimeter of sewage works. Many, such as Rye Meads, Altrincham, Freckleton, Eggington and Swindon, have become famous, but this is probably because one or more competent ornithologists happened to live within walking distance. My local works provides winter sanctuary for a delightful wading bird, the green sandpiper, and like most other works it attracts the occasional rarity.

Black-headed gull

Refuse Tips

To those of us familiar with the hordes of gulls which scavenge around
our refuse tips it is a surprise to find that a foremost Victorian
naturalist, the Rev F. O. Morris, was writing impassioned letters to
The Times in an effort to prevent their extinction. In April 1879 he
wrote complaining that many gulls were being shot for sport, and went
on:

> Another misstatement is that the large gulls eat the young of the rock
> pigeons. The one kind of bird is not of more especial value than the other
> ...the idea of any supposed injury the gulls do by eating fish has long
> since been exploded by the late Commander Knocker R. N., captain of the
> coastguard and eminent ichthyologist, who gave statistics to prove on the
> exact contrary the immense amount of good they do by feeding precisely
> on those very fish which would otherwise destroy the young of the more
> useful kinds in considerable numbers.

A hundred years ago man was threatening the seagulls and now they
seem to be threatening us. They have become competent inland
dwellers, especially out of the breeding season, and nesting on

House sparrow

buildings by herring gulls is on the increase. The reason for their success is not far to seek — it is our throw-away society. Discarded food finds its way to the dumps — fewer of us have fires or boilers on which to burn unwanted food. All this ensures a substantial insect community on the dumps which thus attracts many other species. Here is my list from a small municipal dump for July 1979: black-headed gull, herring gull, lesser black-backed gull, greater black-backed gull, starling, goldfinch, blue tit, great tit, kestrel, rook, crow, jackdaw, magpie, oyster catcher and, a real rarity, a little ringed plover. Plants recorded included red clover, white clover, sweet cicely, knapweed, mint, sneezewort, tomato, self heal, common spotted orchid, pineapple mayweed, yarrow and giant hogweed.

The behaviour of the magpies was of special interest. A group of house sparrows was feeding behind an adjacent wall. The magpie hopped over the wall and walked slowly along the opposite side. It stopped, cocked its head and then jumped quickly onto the wall and dropped onto the sparrows, killed one and ate it with great relish. The magpie story continues. Their nest was sited in a low, isolated hawthorn bush under 6 feet (2 metres) high. Both parents were shot by youths with airguns and all the young died save one. I decided to try an experiment, assisted by some trustworthy youngsters. Instead of 'adopting' the young one and taking it home, we fed it in the nest, after removing its dead siblings. Obviously we do not know if 'maggie' is still alive today, but it did reach the flying stage.

This particular dump is visited by hundreds of rooks which grub about for maggots. It used to be said that a lot of crows together were rooks, and a rook on its own was a crow! This humorous method of distinguishing the two species is only a generalisation, but it does contain a strong element of truth; rooks are much more gregarious than carrion crows. Further points of distinction are that the adult rook has the familiar area of white skin at the base of the bill — and carrion crows do not (nor do young rooks); at all stages the legs of the rook are feathered, giving the impression that it is wearing plus-fours, a feature that can be seen at a distance. Crows have naked legs.

As at the sewage works, occasionally a real rarity turns up and causes great excitement. This little rubbish dump is close to an old quarry and thus is a suitable habitat for the little ringed plover (*Charadrius dubius*). This is yet another example of a creature that has found the habitats created by modern man to its liking. A summer

Young magpie

Rook

visitor, it has bred in England only since 1938, but since then it has
become increasingly common. It is smaller than the more coastal
ringed plover (*Charadrius hiaticula*), being only about 6in (15cm) long,
as against the ringed plover's 7½in (19cm). This can be difficult to
detect at a distance. The ringed plover has a prominent white bar on
the wing clearly seen in flight, a feature totally lacking in *Charadrius
dubius*. Favoured habitats of the little ringed plover are inland rather
than coastal, derelict industrial land rather than pastoral land.

Two 'foreign' plants that have also found man a useful ally in
gaining a first precious foothold in our countryside are the giant
hogweed (*Heracleum mantegazzianum*) and the pineapple mayweed
(*Matricaria matricarioides*). Originally introduced from Russia as an
exotic garden novelty, the giant hogweed is now spreading throughout
the waste places of Britain, often reaching heights approaching 16 feet
(5 metres). As a member of the Umbelliferae or parsley family, its
stems tend to be hollow but I have seen children attempting to climb
hogweed — not an activity to be encouraged since the plant produces a
juice that can cause a painful rash.

Little ringed plover

Pineapple mayweed, or rayless mayweed, is a delightful plant which when crushed gives off a delicate smell of pineapple. It is not a native of Britain and its place of origin is almost certainly Northern Asia. Before the twentieth century it was rare, but with the advent of motor traffic the spread has been dramatic, both in Britain and North America. A close look at the seeds will show how. They are ribbed, and ideally adapted for clinging to muddy surfaces such as boots and car tyres. Some of the seeds germinate quickly but others can lie dormant for long periods, waiting for growing conditions to improve. Again and again we have seen nature's swings-and-roundabouts game, how changes benefit some species but destroy others. This is the way evolution works and it should not always worry us. Gradual change is acceptable on the planet; sudden changes may be more of a problem.

What pleasures await the naturalist studying the aesthetically more pleasing areas of his urban environment?

Parks and Gardens

A neighbour of mine once remarked (in a kindly manner — I think) that my garden was like a tiny wood. His reminded me of a tiny but very tidy park. The days of crowded housing close to industry with no greenery for miles are, thank goodness, receding. Again, trees and grass absorb carbon dioxide, make food with sunlight energy, and as a by-product make the oxygen we need to breathe. The more parks and gardens we have, the more oxygen will enter the atmospheric bank. This account must never be overdrawn.

However, not all trees are able to live in the smoky and dust-filled atmosphere of cities. One species that can is the London plane (*Platanus hybrida*), which I call a compromise tree. Its roots can spread beneath foundations of buildings and roads without causing damage, which must be a city architect's dream. The leaves of any plant are protected by a waterproof cuticle but in the plane this layer is so thick that a smooth surface is produced. Every time it rains the leaves are rinsed free of dust and photosynthetic activity can proceed unhindered. Tree trunks and branches have air-holes, lenticels, in the bark; these can become full of dust and prevent exchange of respiratory gases. In the plane the bark is rough and scaly and periodically it peels off, taking the accumulated dirt with it. If ever a tree was designed to thrive in a modern city, then this is it.

It is, however, an introduced tree, as indeed is the sycamore (*Acer pseudoplatanus*), which is now so much a tree of our parks. Writing in 1597, Gerard said that it was 'a stranger in England, only it groweth in walkes and places of pleasure of noble men, where it especially is planted for the shadowe sake'. In its natural environment the sycamore is a mountain tree and in consequence it has been planted as windbreaks around farms as well as in municipal parks.

The leaves produce a sugary secretion particularly attractive to greenfly (aphids). It forms the base of a food chain beginning with the leaf itself, through the aphid, then small birds, culminating in a top carnivore, such as the tawny owl. When analysing the contents of an owl pellet found in a London park, I found a bird's leg on which was a ring. This was found to have been put on the leg of a great tit ringed close by two years previously. If there had been a field centre in the park, this food chain would have made a most interesting exhibit.

Often as a student I walked the parks of London, binoculars round my neck, and was stopped by people asking for assistance in identifying the animals and plants. All large parks ought to have a

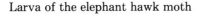

Larva of the elephant hawk moth

small field-studies centre with a warden present during the day. If a professional was thought too expensive, there are many retired people who are excellent naturalists and would be prepared to take on the task. In these days of teacher surplus, could not a young biologist be provided with a mobile classroom in some secluded corner and classes brought there for a field-studies course?

Any resident naturalists will have a job to persuade the authorities to allow parts of the park to grow wild, but this should not prevent them from trying. One plant which should be encouraged is the rosebay willowherb, despite objections from over-tidy officialdom.

You will be able to find this plant (*Chamaenerion angustifolium*) wherever you live in Britain — and unfortunately it often grows where man wants to grow other plants, so is relegated to the status of 'weed', though its flower is most attractive. If it was a rare plant, rosebay would be carefully nurtured and cut-throat competitions would decide who had grown the finest. This perennial 'fireweed' was indeed rare in Britain until about 1860, when it suddenly began to spread, perhaps

Rosebay willowherb

Elephant hawk moth: A adult in flight, B larva, C pupa, D adult at rest

due to some fortuitous genetic change, and it is now found almost everywhere, flowering throughout the summer, colouring large areas of wasteland with a splendid flame of purple light.

Each flowering stem can reach a height of about 6 feet (almost 2 metres). The leaves are arranged in a spiral around the stem and these long crinkly edged lance-like structures are a very popular food with the larvae of many insects, including the elephant hawk moth. The flowers are clustered at the top of the stem in a raceme. After fertilisation the ovary ripens into a long fruit which eventually splits to free masses of feathery cottonwool-like seeds to float about in the wind, often for long distances. The name 'fireweed' probably does not refer to the colour of the plant, but to the fact that *Chamaenerion angustifolium* is the first plant to colonise ground recently ravaged by fire.

The value of one garden to the survival of Britain's wildlife is negligible, but the gardens throughout the length and breadth of the country together provide a vast reservoir for varied flora and fauna. If every gardener set aside a wild corner and allowed rosebay, nettle and other weeds so popular with insects to flourish, and refrained from using harmful chemicals, the wild things would soon flood in. It has

Blue tits

been shown that a thoughtfully laid out garden can attract a higher number of species than either woodland or open fields (though in smaller densities of course) since it combines the attributes of both. Chemical weedkillers and pesticides cause great ecological disruption and garden owners should rely as far as possible on natural food chains. Blue tits and ladybirds, for example, can do much to reduce the aphid populations, starlings eat vast numbers of wireworms and your friendly neighbourhood hedgehog can de-slug a garden in quick time. But from time to time we all need to curb some particularly disruptive element, especially the insect kind, in the garden; this should be done as carefully as possible to avoid chemical overkill and allow the natural food chains to carry on functioning.

Those lucky enough to have larger gardens should read up about garden ponds and the wonderful variety of life which can thrive in and around them. The water louse, dragonfly larvae, caddis fly larvae in their cases made from strips of vegetation, thrive in such areas. Any trees planted should be chosen both for their aesthetic value and with the birds in mind. A bird table and the odd nestbox will prove invaluable, as will the provision of a couple of bird baths. Common

Dragonfly

Dragonfly close-up

Waxwing

species will soon discover the position of these and as birds are creatures of habit soon learn when their 'meal times' are. Less common species such as waxwings, as well as winter visitors of the thrush family, such as redwings and fieldfares, can be attracted by planting suitable shrubs and trees which produce nourishing fruits and berries. Such species include rowan, cotoneaster (very popular with waxwings), berberis, pyracantha (which grows well on north-facing walls) and even honeysuckle, ivy and holly. A crab-apple tree with a good crop of fruit can keep immigrant thrushes going all winter.

One final point on gardens: they are the places where we have a chance of regular contact with living things, more so than in city parks for example. As pointed out earlier it would be a boost for wildlife if field centres were set up in parks, but how much more might we learn from our own gardens if we devoted a little more thought to encouraging wild creatures to share them.

Churchyards

Even today the clamour of everyday life is moderated in churchyards. These areas have been sacred since the city was a town, since the town was a village, since the village was a hamlet and often since the hamlet

243

Whalley Abbey, Lancashire

was a cluster of hovels surrounding a sacred shrine in the primeval woods. Here wild creatures may have been living for generation upon generation in the first-ever nature reserves.

The area taken up by churchyards has been said to be so small that it must be insignificant to our wildlife: but there are something like 16,000 such areas in England alone, constituting in total about 8,000 hectares (20,000 acres) of undisturbed habitat. This figure is far from insignificant. It does not include cemeteries, which although usually consisting of cropped grass and headstones do provide valuable feeding habitat for a variety of species, including winter visitors such as redwings. All the birds require is to be left in peace to feed over the heads of those who rest in peace.

During student days in London I spent many happy hours in the Brompton cemetery, an extensive area with plenty of mature trees and tangled under-shrubs to attract the birds. During a four-year study I recorded 119 species, including on one memorable occasion a waxwing feeding on hawthorn, and on another a mallard's nest containing eight eggs in an old magpie's nest about 15 feet (5 metres) off the ground.

My work at Brompton concentrated on one species in particular, the

Churchyard at Billington, Lancashire

Jay

jay. Masses of acorns brought from my home in Cumbria and spread upon the ground could be guaranteed to bring the jays, often as many as eight, to feed. They are amongst the most intelligent of birds and soon learned where to come and at what time. Hidden behind huge marble mausoleums, which sprout like autumn fungi around Brompton, I was able to sit quietly and observe, the traffic sounds from the Fulham road almost totally muted. All went well apart from one embarrassing session trying to answer searching questions from a London copper. A lady had apparently reported me for spying on her. My field notebook convinced him that I was 'respectably nuts' instead of 'criminally peculiar'. I wonder to this day how the lady saw me without me seeing her and what she was doing that she didn't want me to see: it doesn't say much for my woodcraft.

On one occasion I had just settled down behind a tombstone when I noticed a jay approaching the smoking stub of a cigarette lying on the path. To my surprise the bird picked up the cigarette in its bill and began to rub the still-smoking stub into the feathers beneath its wing. I was thrilled at being treated to an exhibition of a phenomenon which ornithologists call anting. Anting is still not fully understood, but it is thought that by rubbing an ant on the feathers the formic acid produced by the insect may kill or repel parasites. Many of the passeriformes (perching birds) have been observed anting, either with actual ants or in smoke, which was obviously what my jay was up to. Some ornithologists have expressed doubts as to the effectiveness of this process. However the work of Vsevolod B. Dubinin has thrown light on the question: a microscopic investigation of the stomach contents of over 20,000 feather mites showed that they ate fat-droplets from their host's plumage, possibly reducing its ability to repel water. He then treated the mites with formic acid removed from ants and found that out of 732 mites 253 were dead within 12 hours. A control group of 758 kept without being treated had only 3 deaths. Here, it seems, is the rationale behind the anting behaviour.

Many churchyards have a gnarled and ancient yew tree (*Taxus baccata*), its evergreen leaves often hiding the secretive little goldcrest, the smallest of our resident birds. It has been said that these trees were planted to provide timber for long bows in times of military crisis. In 1815 Wordsworth alluded to this.

> There is a yew-tree, pride of Lorton Vale,
> Which to this day stands single in the midst
> Of its own darkness as it stood of yore,
> Not loth to furnish weapons for the bands.

This idea is now discounted since staves for the traditional long bow were imported. Indeed in the middle ages the authorities ensured such a supply by imposing an import tax of a certain measure of yew timber to accompany each barrel of foreign wine.

The origin of the name yew is subject to debate. Some say it derives from the Welsh *yw*, and if this is so then the tree is unique in being the only one to retain its Celtic name, meaning 'it is'; compare the Hebrew name for God, Yahweh, meaning 'I am'! Others argue that the Celtic *yewar* means evergreen head, an accurate description. The scientific name could come either from Greek or Latin: if the Greek, then it could indicate the neat arrangement of the leaves; if Latin, the *toxicum* means a poison, and certainly the foliage is poisonous. In 1897 Lowe investigated the poison, using the experimental technique accepted at the time — he bravely tried it on himself. He found that his pulse was slowed and his blood pressure sharply raised following even very slight doses. Having already disposed of the bow-and-arrow theory it

Yew

is suggested that yews may have been planted in English churchyards just because they were poisonous to cattle and thus farmers would keep their stock out of consecrated ground.

The history of the churchyard yew, however, remains obscure. To Neolithic man religion was doubtless a gory ritual and outdoor gatherings would have been held beneath long-living sacred trees; these provided shelter and, more significantly, permanence. When man learned to fell trees he would have left these ancient giants for fear of angering long-established gods. When Christianity arrived the religious groves were taken over and eventually churches constructed close to them; credence is lent to this proposed sequence of events by the great antiquity of many of our churchyard yews. A yew can live upwards of 1,000 years and the young tree is able to grow from the dead trunk of its parent. Go into an ancient churchyard, find a yew tree, sit beneath its shade: consider that the great-great-grandparent of this tree grew tall and spread wide in the old wild woods, provided shelter for wolf and wildcat, pine marten and polecat, wild boar and badger. Here then is the one remaining remnant of Britain's ancient woods, retained at the insistence of man's religious need. We have now come full circle and considered what man has done with nature's tapestry and how at last he is learning to appreciate that he can never defeat her and survive himself. He is but a small part of her scheme, and must operate within it.

Bibliography

General

Bennett, D. P. and Humphries, D. A., *Introduction to Field Biology* (Arnold, 1974)

Burton, John, *Conservation of Wildlife* (Blackie, 1974)

Clapham, A. R. (etc.), *Excursion Flora of the British Isles* (Cambridge, 1968)

Corbet, G. B. and Southern, H. N. (Eds), *Handbook of British Mammals* (Blackwell, 1977)

Cramp, S. (Chief Ed), *Handbook of the Birds of Europe, the Middle East and North Africa*, 2 Vols (Oxford, 1977, 1980)

Edington, J. M. and M. A., *Ecology and Environmental Planning* (Chapman and Hall, 1977)

Fitter, M. and R., *The Penguin Dictionary of Natural History* (Penguin 1967, 1978)

Hollom, P. A. D., *The Popular Handbook of British Birds* (Witherby, 1968)

Kirkman, J., *The British Bird Book* (Jack, 1911)

Sharrock, J. T. R. (Ed), *Atlas of Breeding Birds in Britain and Ireland* (BTO/ Poyser, 1976)

Sheail, J., *Nature in Trust* (Blackie, 1976)

South, R., *The Moths of the British Isles* (Warne, 1973)

**Chapter 1 Woodland; the Basic Habitat and
Chapter 2 The Woodland Web**

Blatchford, N., *Your Book of Forestry* (Faber, 1980)

Condry, W., *Woodlands* (Collins, 1974)

Cousens, J., *An Introduction to Woodland Ecology* (Oliver and Boyd, 1974)

Deal, W., *A Guide to Forest Holidays in Great Britain and Ireland* (David and Charles, 1976)

Edlin, H. L., *Trees, Woods and Men* (Collins, 1956)

Fiennes, R., *The Order of Wolves* (Hamish Hamilton, 1976)

Hickin, N., *The Natural History of an English Forest* (Hutchinson, 1971)

Institute of Terrestrial Ecology, *Native Pinewoods of Scotland* (1977)

Kosch, A., *The Young Specialist Looks at Trees* (Burke, 1972)

Leathart, S., *Exploring Woodlands and Forests* (EP Publishing, 1978)

Lopez, Barry H., *Of Wolves and Men* (Dent, 1979)

Manning, S. A., *The Woodland World* (World's Work, 1972)

Mitchell, A., *A Field Guide to the Trees of Britain and Northern Europe* (Collins, 1974)

Neal, E. G., *Woodland Ecology* (Heinemann, 1953, 1969)

Pennington, W., *The History of British Vegetation* (English Universities Press, 1974)

Perring F., and Morris, B. (Eds), *The British Oak* (Classey, 1974)
Perrins, C. M., *British Tits* (Collins, 1979)
Rackham, B., *Trees and Woodlands in the British Landscape* (Dent, 1976)
Ryle, G., *Forest Service* (David and Charles, 1969)
Simms, E., *Woodland Birds* (Collins, 1971)
Tansley, A. G., *The British Islands and their Vegetation* (Cambridge University Press, 1953)
Tubbs, C., *The New Forest* (David and Charles, 1968)
Watling, H., *Identification of the Larger Fungi* (Hulton)
White, G., *The Natural History of Selborne*
Wilks, J. H., *Trees of the British Isles in History and Legend* (Muller, 1972)

Chapter 3 The Hedge
Brown, L., *British Birds of Prey* (Collins, 1976)
Hansen, E., *Life in the Hedgerow* (Wayland, 1978)
Jennings, T., *The World of the Hedge* (Faber, 1978)
Pollard, Hooper and Moore, *Hedges* (Collins, 1974)
Wilkinson, G., *Epitaph for the Elm* (Hutchinson, 1978)
Wilson, R., *The Hedgerow Book* (David and Charles, 1979)

Chapter 4 Fields and Farms
Boyd, A. W., *Country Diary of a Cheshire Man* (Collins, 1945)
Burrows, R., *Wild Fox* (David and Charles, 1968)
Carr, R., *English Fox Hunting, a History* (Weidenfeld, 1976)
Cowan, D., *The Wild Rabbit* (Blandford, 1980)
Hubbard, C. E., *Grasses* (Pelican, 1968)
Jackman, L., *The Field* (Evans, 1972)
Lockley, R. M., *The Private Life of the Rabbit* (Deutsch, 1964)
MacGillivray, W., *Manual of British Birds*, (Adam Scott, 1846)
Mellanby, K., *The Mole* (Collins, 1971)
Russel, Sir John, *The World of the Soil* (Collins, 1957)
Spencer, K. G., *The Lapwing in Britain* (Oliver and Boyd, 1953)
Taylor, C., *Fields in the English Landscape* (Dent, 1975)
Zeigler, P., *The Black Death* (Collins, 1969)

Chapter 5 Fresh Water — Supply and Demand
Angel, H., *The World of a Stream* (Faber, 1976)
Balfour Brown, *British Water Beetles* (Ray Society, 1940–58)
Batten, L. A. (Ed), *The Bird Watcher's Year* (Poyser, 1973)
Clegg, J., *The Freshwater Life of the British Isles* (Warne, 1952)
Cooke, A., *The Birds of Grafham Water* (Nature Conservancy Council, 1979)
Eastman, Rosemary, *The Kingfisher* (Collins, 1969)
Freshwater Biological Association (Scientific Publications, Ferry House, Windermere)
Harrison, J. and Grant, P., *Thames Transformed* (Deutsch, 1976)
Haslam, S. M., *River Plants* (Cambridge University Press, 1978)
Macan, T. T., *Freshwater Ecology* (Longmans, 1963)
Macan, T. T. and Worthington, E. B., *Life in Lakes and Rivers* (Collins, 1951)
Mills, D. H., *An Introduction to Freshwater Ecology* (Oliver and Boyd, 1972)
Russell, R., *Rivers* (David and Charles, 1978)
Tanner, M. F., *Water Space Amenity Commission Report* (1980)
Ticehurst, N. F., *The Mute Swan in England* (1957)
Wheeler, A., *The Tidal Thames* (Routledge, 1979)

Chapter 6 Mountains and Moorlands

Brown, L., *British Birds of Prey* (Collins, 1976)
Chalmers, P. R., *Deerstalking* (Sportsman's Library, 1935)
Condry, W., *The World of a Mountain* (Faber, 1973)
Darling, F. and Morton Boyd, J., *The Highlands and Islands* (Collins, 1964)
Darlington, A., *The Natural History of Mountains and Moorlands* (Hodder, 1980)
Leutcher, A., *The Ecology of Mountains* (Franklin Watts, 1978)
Nethersole Thompson, D. and M., *Greenshanks* (Poyser, 1979)
Ogilvie-Grant, W. R., *Handbook to the Game Birds* (Lloyds Natural History, 2 vols, 1896)
Pearsall, W. H., *Mountains and Moorlands* (Collins, 1950)
Plant Communities of the Scottish Highlands (Nature Conservancy Monograph No. 1, 1963)
The Hidden Killers (RSPB, 1980)
Watson, D., *The Hen Harrier* (Poyser, 1977)

Chapter 7 The Coastline

Angel, H., *The World of an Estuary* (Faber, 1975)
Barnes, R. S. K., *Estuarine Biology* (Arnold, 1974)
Chapman, V. J., *Coastal Vegetation* (Pergamon, 1976)
Eddison, J., *The World of a Changing Coastline* (Faber, 1979)
Gibson-Hill, C. A., *British Sea Birds* (Witherby, 1947)
Jackman, L., *The Beach* (Evans, 1974)
Maxwell, G., *Ring of Bright Water* (Longman, 1960)
Tuck, G., *Field Guide to the Seabirds of Britain and the World* (Collins, 1978)

Chapter 8 Urban Wildlife

Ardley, N., *Birds of Towns* (Almark, 1975)
Berrisford, J., *The Wild Garden* (Faber, 1973)
Chinery, M., *The Natural History of the Garden* (Collins, 1977)
Coombs, F., *The Crows* (Batsford, 1978)
Genders, R., *Wildlife in the Garden* (Faber, 1976)
Goodden, R., *British Butterflies — A Field Guide* (David and Charles, 1978)
Goodwin, D., *Birds of Man's World* (Cornell University Press, 1978)
Johnston, D., *Roman Roads in Britain* (Spurbooks, 1979)
Linssen, E. F., *Observer's Book of Common Insects and Spiders* (Warne, 1973)
Mabey, R., *Street Flowers* (Kestrel, 1976)
McKnight, Hugh, *Shell Book of Inland Waterways* (David and Charles, 1978)
Morris, F. O., *Letters to* The Times *about Birds* (Poole, 1879)
Owen, D., *The Naturalist History of Towns and Gardens* (Hodder, 1978)
Simms, E., *Birds of Town and Suburb* (Collins, 1975)
Simms, E., *British Thrushes* (Collins, 1978)
Simms, E., *The Public Life of the Street Pigeon* (Hutchinson, 1979)
Soper, T., *Wildlife Begins at Home* (David and Charles, 1975)
Taylor, C., *Roads and Tracks of Britain* (Dent, 1979)
Wilmore, S. B., *Crows, Jays and Ravens* (David and Charles, 1977)

Acknowledgements

During the preparation of this book I have received generous assistance from many sources. I am particularly grateful to Anthony Colin who produced the line drawings, cheerfully adapting to my many changes of mind. Where my own collection of photographs proved inadequate Bill Wilkinson and Robert Howe, both more skilled in the art than I, made their own extensive collections available to me. To the RSPB I extend my thanks for the picture of the pole trap and also to David Crossley who allowed me to use his photograph of a northern moorland.

With regard to the manuscript itself I am indebted to the editorial staff of David and Charles and also to E. K. Dunn who corrected errors both of style and fact. My final thanks must go to all members of my family who helped to ease the pain of the book's long gestation period, but especially to my wife who willingly typed the manuscript direct from my handwriting and kept cheerful at a time when lesser mortals may well have despaired. Remaining faults in the work are purely my own responsibility.

Ashdale, Burnley
August 1980.

Index

Numbers in *italics* refer to illustrations

254

255